The Power of
Three

Remembering the Tools of Creation

Yvette Sheppard,
Jasmine Sheppard &
Alexa Sheppard

BALBOA.PRESS
A DIVISION OF HAY HOUSE

Balboa Press books may be ordered through booksellers or by contacting:

Balboa Press
A Division of Hay House
1663 Liberty Drive
Bloomington, IN 47403
www.balboapress.co.uk
UK TFN: 0800 0148647 (Toll Free inside the UK)
UK Local: (02) 0369 56325 (+44 20 3695 6325 from outside the UK)

Because of the dynamic nature of the Internet, any web addresses or links contained in this book may have changed since publication and may no longer be valid. The views expressed in this work are solely those of the author and do not necessarily reflect the views of the publisher, and the publisher hereby disclaims any responsibility for them.

The author of this book does not dispense medical advice or prescribe the use of any technique as a form of treatment for physical, emotional, or medical problems without the advice of a physician, either directly or indirectly. The intent of the author is only to offer information of a general nature to help you in your quest for emotional and spiritual well-being. In the event you use any of the information in this book for yourself, which is your constitutional right, the author and the publisher assume no responsibility for your actions.

Any people depicted in stock imagery provided by Getty Images are models, and such images are being used for illustrative purposes only. Certain stock imagery © Getty Images.

Print information available on the last page.

ISBN: 978-1-9822-8642-2 (sc)
ISBN: 978-1-9822-8644-6 (hc)
ISBN: 978-1-9822-8643-9 (e)

Balboa Press rev. date: 09/29/2022

Contents

PREFACE

We each received spiritual messages from our higher selves during the creation of this book. Throughout the process, it has evolved in so many ways to become the book that you are reading today. We have been consciously creating our lives for as long as we can remember, and we continue to learn and expand our knowledge to this day. We knew that this book would be a collation of our knowledge and all of the tools we use to create our own beautiful lives. It is our intention that this book will serve as a way of helping you to take back your own power and remember the tools of creation. We know this will be your go-to book when you need a gentle reminder of the tools to focus your power in order to create the reality you desire.

We have intentionally used the power of three on many occasions and have come to know the power that it holds. By harnessing the power of three, we have been able to amplify our knowledge and wisdom to create a comprehensive, multifaceted book just for you.

Acknowledgements

With special appreciation to our dear friend and spiritual intuitive, Tracy Newton. Your intuitive reading provided us with the motivation that we needed to start writing this book.

A special thanks to Kathleen Taylor (Mum/Mamma) and Great Aunt Pamela Gibson for their unequivocal support, encouragement and patience whilst waiting for the completed book.

To an amazing husband and Dad, Tony, and wonderful son and brother, Aaron, for being so generous in giving us time and space to create our vision.

A huge shout out to all of our friends, family and clients who have shared our excitement and anticipation for the release of our book.

Finally, with gratitude to May Arado and the team at Balboa Press for their incredible support and expertise during the publishing process.

1

Introduction

There is no time like the present to remember what a powerful creator you are. You have the innate power and ability to create your reality and manifest all that you desire. You are creating your life, whether you are consciously aware of it or not. If you want to change your life for the better, you must take responsibility for it. The process of creating your life is also known as manifestation, and we will refer to this process as both manifestation and creation throughout this book. You cocreate your reality with the Universe, Divine Source, God, Source Energy, Source, the Divine Creator. All of these are titles of the same energy. Use whichever title resonates the most with you when cocreating your reality.

In this book we will share with you an incredible spiritual download of information known as The Nine Code of Fidelity[a]. The Nine Code of Fidelity is a nine-stage process to guide you through manifesting anything you desire. By using the tools found within this book, you can easily create your dream life. This book will provide you with tools to help you remember how to focus your power and use it to create your reality. The process of creation is supposed to be fun. So have fun with it and use the tools that you feel drawn to and resonate with. We are so proud to be with you on your journey of awakening your power within and remembering the tools of creation.

2

TAKING BACK YOUR POWER

It is so important that you recognise the power you have within yourself. You are a powerful multidimensional being having a lifetime in a human body. Unfortunately, for most of us, we forgot this when we came to Earth and became conditioned by social norms throughout our childhood. Perhaps you were discouraged from spiritual connection as a child and told that it is all woo-woo. So over the years you gave your power away to all the people in the world who want to tell you who you are and what you can and cannot do. They tell you that you shouldn't question the narrative, even when you have this deep inner knowing that something is amiss. There is nothing I love more than the saying "do your own research". You wouldn't blindly follow someone telling you to invest in a particular asset without doing your own research first and checking in with your intuition. So why would you not do the same for any narratives you are fed?

I can imagine at some point in your life you, have had someone impose their own limitations and mindset upon you. Did you get told what your path in life would be at school or by your parents? You will go to school, get an education, perhaps go to university, and then work a nine-to-five job for the rest of your life. Until, of course, you retire, and only then can you have complete freedom over how you spend your time. Sadly, a lot of people find themselves a slave to this system—working a job that they dislike merely to pay the bills. My intention here is not to say that working a nine-to-five job or working for someone else is a bad thing if you resonate with it. The key is that you resonate with the work you are doing and love to show up to it every day. Perhaps you were told that you would never be able to move to a big house in the city because you would never be able to afford it. That's how the other half live, not us. Again, this is someone else imposing their own limitations and mindset upon you. You are more than capable of creating your own life, so settle for nothing less than your greatest desires in every aspect. Whatever it is, you have the power to bring it into your reality.

Stop putting people or things on a pedestal and take yourself out of the box you have allowed others to put you in. You have the power within you. You are a limitless being.

Use Your Intuition

I cannot stress enough how essential it is that you learn to use and trust your intuition. You may have heard people use the expression "go with your gut". This refers to trusting your intuition, and your intuition comes from your higher self. Your higher self is the version of you that is your soul consciousness. It is a combination of you from all of your lifetimes. Essentially, by trusting your intuition, you are placing your trust in your higher self and cultivating inner self-trust. It will always guide you to the decision or place that serves your highest good if you choose to follow it. Most people are discouraged from listening to their intuition and encouraged to search for answers outside of themselves or using their rational mind. You have all of the answers that you need within—all you need to do is ask. There are many ways that your intuition can communicate with you. It may feel like an urge or pull towards something, a thought, a feeling, a deep inner knowing, or it may even be in the form of images. By listening, you can determine what it is telling you.

How Do You Start Listening and Tuning into Your Intuition?

Start by asking your higher self questions about insignificant things first. With bigger decisions, your mind is more likely to get involved and analyse the situation. For instance, you could go somewhere that you are familiar with, and when you reach a crossroads, ask your higher self which direction you should take and see which way you feel you should go. To reiterate, this could be anything from an urge, to a thought, to a feeling—to name but a few.

As you begin to tune into and trust your intuition with smaller, more insignificant things, you will gain confidence in your ability to do this for the bigger things that your rational mind is more likely to want to analyse.

Even when you are used to trusting your intuition, there may still be occasions when your rational mind gets involved, and you choose to do the opposite of your intuition. A company approached me once to offer an advertising opportunity for my business. I checked in with my intuition to see if I should take this opportunity and received a strong *no* feeling. However, my rational mind started to analyse this feeling and attributed it to a dislike of the institution involved. So I went ahead with the advertising and, of course, swiftly realised it was not the correct decision. In instances like this, it's important that you acknowledge the lesson that you have learnt from the situation.

How Do You Tell the Difference Between Intuition and Fear?

First of all, growth can be scary because you are expanding into the unknown. For instance, you may have a fear of speaking in front of a large group of people, but if your intuition is guiding you to do it, you shouldn't let fear stop you. You need to feel the fear and do it anyway. Your intuition will always guide you in the correct direction that serves your highest good. By working through the fear, you are unlocking the next steps in your growth. Of course, your intuition will also tell you if something is not correct for you. But how do you determine the difference between the fear that is necessary to work through for growth and your intuitive gut feeling telling you that something is not right for you? Intuition will feel light, expansive, unemotional, and calm in the body. It is an effortless knowing if something is correct or not without any reasoning. On the other hand, fear is a heavy, constricted, anxious, and worried feeling in the body. Fear also arises as analytical thoughts in the mind, such as what might happen in the future as a result of the decision. Intuition is centred in the present moment and therefore does not produce these types of thoughts; it is an inner knowing. Despite this, after you have received your intuitive feeling, your rational mind may begin to analyse the feeling and produce such thoughts. Trust your intuition. Your intuition will never fail you. The more you learn to tune into and trust your intuition, the more you will build inner self-trust and be able to follow your intuition, even in the face of analytical thoughts from your logical mind.

With each tool in this book, use your intuition to feel whether you resonate with it or not. If you do, go ahead and use it to help focus your power within to create your desires.

3

Universal Laws

When you think about the universal laws with regards to manifestation, the one that comes to mind is, of course, the Law of Attraction. That is, that which you place your thoughts and attention on is manifested into your physical reality. Like attracts like. It is the first universal law that I came to know in association with manifestation years ago through the book *The Secret to Teen Power* by Paul Harrington. There are, however, many universal laws which all contribute to the process of manifestation. Whether you are consciously manifesting your reality or not, the laws are still in motion, so use them for your benefit. Let us now take a deeper look into twelve of the universal laws.

Law of Divine Oneness

This law states that we are all one, connected to each other. I like to think of it as we are all created from the same Source Energy, and we all have that same spark within us. We are spiritual beings having an incarnation in a human body. We are all a part of the collective consciousness; a shared collection of knowledge and experience that everyone can access and contribute to. As humans, we are a microcosm of the macrocosm—the universe. Whilst we are creating our own individual realities, we are also contributing to the creation of our collective reality and experience of the world through the collective consciousness. Taking part in group meditation is a great way to send love and positive energy out into the collective consciousness to help shape our collective reality.

As we are all one, from the same Source Energy, we can have anything anyone else has in life. Success and fulfilment beyond your wildest dreams? Of course! Abundance in every aspect of your life? You bet! I love to see people in my life achieving what I desire to achieve. Whether that be moving into a new home, getting their dream job or creating a successful business. It reassures you through the Law of Divine Oneness that this is also possible for you.

Law of Vibration

Everything has a vibration and frequency that it emits out into the world. It is easy to throw around these words when discussing manifestation, but what do they mean, and how are they related?

Well, everything in this world from humans to animals, to the coffee table in your living room consists of microscopic atoms that are vibrating in a constant motion. This movement is what we refer to as a vibration. The speed at which the vibration occurs is referred to as the frequency. More specifically, the frequency is the number of cycles per second given in hertz (Hz). The higher the frequency, the more cycles per second, and thus a higher value in Hz.

For example, in figure 1, by counting the number of cycles that occurred over one second, we can determine the low frequency wave is 4 Hz compared to the high frequency wave of 8 Hz.

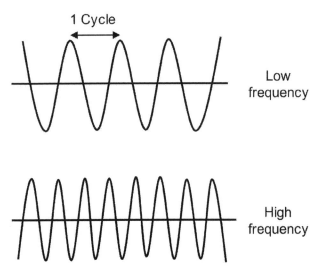

1 Cycle

Low frequency

High frequency

Figure 1. Representation of Frequency. Shown over a timespan of one second.

The saying goes, you raise your frequency to that which you desire to manifest, and you will become a match to it to bring it into your reality. Surround yourself with high frequency people whom you would aspire to be, as you become a product of those that you spend the most time with. This also goes for those you follow on social media, whose content you consume on a daily basis.

In order to utilise the Law of Vibration, I like to think about the emotions that the version of myself I wish to embody would be feeling. If my intention is to manifest financial freedom, the version of myself that already has financial freedom would not embody lower frequency emotions such as fear and shame. She would embody higher frequency emotions such as gratitude, joy and freedom. I would then consider what I could do in the present to elevate my frequency to feel such emotions and let go of any lower frequency emotions that no longer serve me to become vibrationally aligned.

It is possible for you to be in vibrational alignment with something to bring it into your reality but be unable to keep it there. Perhaps this could be due to unhealed underlying beliefs or a lesson from a soul agreement. For example, if you readily attract money but cannot seem to retain your wealth, you may need to do work around healing your underlying money beliefs. Alternatively, you may have a soul agreement lesson, such as a lesson to learn to release fear, insecurity or self-worth surrounding money.

Law of Correspondence

There is a relationship between the way you think and view yourself in your inner world and the way you experience the world on the outside. Your reality is created through your repeated subconscious patterns, beliefs and thoughts, which in turn directly reflect what you experience in your outer world.

If you have inner thoughts of happiness, joy and self-worth, you will reflect this in your outer reality. Equally, if you have inner thoughts of low self-worth, hate and anger, this will be reflected in your outer reality. You must be willing to change your state in your inner world if you wish to change your outer world.

The Law of Correspondence can be used to discover limiting patterns and beliefs to allow you to deal with them accordingly. Something that triggers you in another person is actually a reflection of something you reject in yourself; an unhealed, subconscious self-limiting belief. For example, you may feel anger towards someone speaking their mind and discover that, as a child, you were repeatedly told not to speak up and be quiet. In turn, this resulted in you suppressing this aspect of yourself into your subconscious, as a belief that speaking your mind is wrong. It is crucial when you are triggered to take a moment to acknowledge what you are feeling and subsequently dive into why you feel that way in order to heal. If you continuously ignore the emotions that arise when you are triggered, they will just continue to manifest in other situations in your life until they are addressed.

Law of Attraction

As previously mentioned, the Law of Attraction is perhaps the most addressed universal law in the manifestation space. This law states that like attracts like, and whatever you place your thoughts and attention on and believe will happen is manifested into your physical reality. Align your thoughts with what you desire to manifest as where attention goes, energy flows. As you align yourself, you will take inspired actionable steps toward the manifestation of your desires (Law of Inspired Action).

If you focus on the positive aspects, you will receive more positivity. Whereas, if you focus on the negative aspects, you will receive more of that. Your thoughts become words, and your words are spells. Your subconscious mind does not have a sense of humour, so ensure you use your thoughts and words wisely.

It is not to say that if lower frequency emotions arise, you should ignore and suppress these emotions. You must do the necessary work to feel, address and heal the underlying cause of these emotions.

"I am" is one of the most powerful phrases you can use for manifestation, as what follows is what you will attract. I am that I am. I am healthy; I am wealthy; I am abundant in all areas of my life; I am happy; I am loved—to name just a few examples. You can use "I am" affirmations as a technique to reprogram your subconscious mind.

In relation to the Law of Vibration, in order to harness the Law of Attraction, it is important to vibrate at the same level as what you desire to manifest. A phrase I love is that "the Law of

Attraction is the Law of Vibration in action", because it is just that!

Law of Inspired Action

In order to assist the manifestation process, you must take inspired action towards your goals. The inspiration for such action may come in the form of a strong intuitive urge, idea or epiphany. It may not make logical sense at the time, but trust the process and take the inspired action.

Pay attention to any synchronicities you see, as these are messages from the Universe. You may see repeating numbers known as angel numbers in your environment. For example, 11:11 on the clock or 888 on number plates have associated meanings and messages that we will delve into in Chapter 11: Inspired Action, Signs and Synchronicities.

It is great practice to create space for guidance using tools such as meditation so that the Universe can communicate with you. I often ask the Universe for guidance but neglect to give the space for answers. My guides were a little – shall we say – frustrated about this. So, ensure that you give yourself time and space to hear the answers and follow the guidance.

Law of Perpetual Transmutation of Energy

Energetically everything is in a constant state of fluctuation and motion. Energy can neither be created nor destroyed but rather transmuted. Water, for example, may be the energetic state of a solid, liquid or a gas. In all states the energy has taken on a different form, but it still exists.

In this way, lower frequencies can be transmuted to higher frequencies. It follows that you are able to change your frequency if you so intend. It is possible to increase a low frequency through positive actions which in turn leads to positive thoughts. If I am feeling low frequency, I will often listen to high frequency music that makes me feel good. This in turn triggers the transmutation of energy to a higher frequency.

Thoughts become your reality through the Law of Perpetual Transmutation of Energy. When you consistently place your thoughts and intention on your desires, you are directing the transmutation of the energy of the thought to manifest into your physical reality. If you desire your dream job, but subconsciously, you believe you are not worthy of it, you will act out of this feeling and create conflict between what you desire and how you subconsciously feel. As you act according to your subconscious belief, it leads to you attracting situations that are in alignment with the feeling of unworthiness. The erratic energy makes it difficult for the Universe to transmute the energy into the physical form you desire. You must do the inner work on the self-limiting belief and reframe the belief so that your thoughts and actions reflect the belief of worthiness. This consistent energy can then be transmuted into your physical reality.

Law of Cause and Effect

The Law of Cause and Effect states that for every cause, there is an effect and vice versa. As such, for every action, there will be a reaction. The nature of the outcome depends on your thoughts and vibration, as this determines the action you take.

If your actions surround generosity, gratitude and love, you will receive more of them in your life as a result of your actions. Whereas, if your actions surround negativity and ungratefulness, you will receive more of them.

If you practice gratitude every day, you are putting positivity and gratitude out into the world, and there must be a positive reaction to your action. This practice brings more things to be grateful for into your life, including your desires. So even though you do not always see the effects of your manifestation practices straight away, stick with them because there must be a resulting outcome to your action.

It is also your decision how you choose to act and respond to a situation. If you encounter a negative situation, you can choose to respond with love and positivity. In turn, this will bring more love and positivity into your life.

Law of Compensation

This law states you receive back what you put out to the Universe in equal quantities. The more effort you put in, the more you are compensated. The more you give, the more you receive. You are compensated for your thoughts, intentions and actions. If you give money, you will receive money. If you have thoughts and beliefs of abundance, you will receive abundance in your life. If you give love and happiness, you will receive love and happiness. This compensation may not happen instantly or in the way you expect, but this law gives you the reassurance that it will.

There are so many ways you can be compensated from the Universe. Remember, no way is too crazy or out there. Let go of how you think it might happen. You must be open to all of the many possibilities. Several years ago, Jasmine and I completed tasks on an online casino, and we both won money. Now I am not telling you that if you go out and gamble, that you will receive money. I simply want to highlight that neither of us would have ever considered that this would have been how we would receive money from the Universe. The Universe works in amazing and mysterious ways, and it is so important to keep yourself open to the limitless ways of receiving.

Law of Relativity

This law relates to the inherent neutrality of everything in this world. We undergo societal conditioning, along with ancestral beliefs and trauma, which lead us to believe how we should perceive situations.

The same situation you view one way may be viewed another way by someone else. Therefore, there is always more than one perspective on any one situation. When in isolation, everything is neutral. It is our perception and perspective of the situation, in comparison to something else, that we then lose this sense of neutrality. Take the situation, for instance, where someone feels ungrateful for their car. They feel this way because they are comparing their car to someone else's car, which is newer and sportier. Rather than feeling ungrateful, they should focus on all of the good aspects and feel grateful for their situation without comparing it to the situation of others.

Law of Polarity

Everything in this world has an opposite. Whether it is good and evil, light and dark, up and down, love and hate or hot and cold. Opposites are necessary for us to be able to decern the meaning of our experience at each end of the spectrum. We can use these relationships to gain clarity on what it is we actually want to experience. We don't know the experience of one without having experienced the other; they are two sides of the same coin. Would you know success if you had not experienced failure? Would you know light if you had not experienced dark? Would you know hot if you had not experienced cold?

The Law of Polarity can indicate why your goal is not manifesting into your reality. You may be focusing on success in your career, for instance, whilst you have underlying subconscious self-limiting beliefs of failure. These self-limiting beliefs influence the energy behind your intentions. It follows that the underlying energy behind your intention is aligned with the opposite polarity of what you desire. So, as you are consciously focused on one polarity, you are also subconsciously focused on the opposite polarity. In turn they can cancel each other out. It is important to heal these self-limiting beliefs so that your emotions and energy behind your intention align with what you desire to experience—in this case, with success. This allows you to use your energy to manifest your desires in the most efficient way possible.

Law of Rhythm

Cycles are a naturally occurring part of the universe and can be seen in our everyday lives, flowing and moving constantly. You may notice the flow of the changing seasons, the cycle of life, the way you breathe in and out, the movement of the tides, the rise and fall of economic markets—to name a few. As everything is in this constant movement and change, it is important to embrace the change in your life. Focus on the positive aspects of each phase of life. It follows that if you find a particular part of your life difficult, know that it will change because that is the Law of Rhythm.

Law of Gender

All things have both divine masculine and divine feminine energy within them. The divine masculine energy has qualities which include logic, structure, assertiveness, confidence, boundaries and taking action. The divine feminine energy has qualities including intuition, inner reflection, creativity, and being more passive, compassionate, kind and forgiving.

It is important to reach a balance of the divine masculine and divine feminine energies that is correct for you. If the balance is too far towards the divine masculine energy, or the divine feminine energy for you, you may feel disharmony.

4

The Nine Code of Fidelity*

The Nine Code of Fidelity® came to me as a spiritual download from my higher self and guides one morning, and it became abundantly clear that this information should be shared with you all through this book. As I was beginning to wake up, I was shown a vision. I was in a tunnel of light moving quickly—similar to what I imagine the inside of a portal or a wormhole to look like—and I heard "The Nine Code of Fidelity" repeated over and over again. I felt this was a process for manifestation. Words, which I felt were the stages of The Nine Code of Fidelity, started to fly past me. I then started to hear "The Nine Code" being repeated as if to say, "this is really important information you need to wake up and write it down". There was then a sudden vibration at the bottom of my bed, just below my feet, which made me wake up and write it down.

As the words of the stages moved past me so quickly in the vision, I couldn't remember what they were. Yvette used a hypnosis technique to access my higher self and recall the stages. During this session, we retrieved all nine stages and the order in which they occur.

You may be wondering, just as I was when I received this information, what does fidelity actually mean? Fidelity isn't a word I use frequently. It can either mean "Faithfulness to a person, cause, or belief, demonstrated by continuing loyalty and support. Or the degree of exactness with which something is copied or reproduced" (Oxford Languages). In this context, I feel that it means faithfulness to the process of The Nine Code of Fidelity, which, if used accurately, allows you to manifest all of your desires.

The Nine Code of Fidelity is a collection of nine stages of the manifestation process following the initial conception of a thought through to it being made manifest in physical reality. Following the process of the nine stages allows you to apply it to anything that you desire to manifest. You will be able to use a variety of the tools found throughout this book to assist you at each stage.

As you are reading this book, I am sure that there are many things that you desire to manifest in life. Consider the one thing you desire to manifest the most right now and keep this in mind as we move through the stages of The Nine Code of Fidelity[a].

Align

The first stage is to align. You must align yourself with the version of yourself that you wish to embody. The version of yourself that is currently living the life you are manifesting. Past, present and future all occur simultaneously—time is a man-made illusion. Everything actually happens in the present moment—the now. Think about it this way. You have gone on holiday abroad, and there is a five-hour time difference between you and your family at home. When you call them at 13:00 in the time zone that you are currently in, it's 18:00 for your family at home. Despite this, you don't view them as being in the future. You view them as being in the present moment, the now, just the same as you. Whether you currently view something as being in the past, present or future depends on your perspective in relation to the occurrence of the event. You are actually always in the present when the event occurs. You could go as far as to say that past and future do not exist; they are merely illusions.

As there are timelines for every possible situation, there is already a version of you that is living the life of your desires in the present moment. That may be a you that has financial freedom, lives in your dream home or has perfect health. The possibilities are endless. If you can think of it, then there is already a version of yourself living it now. By aligning with that version of yourself, you are ultimately aligning with your desires.

So how do you align with that version of yourself?

Ask yourself the following:

1. What emotions do they embody, having received what you desire?

    *   Do they have joy and gratitude for their life?
    *   Do they perhaps feel an abundance of love?
    *   Do they feel freedom over how they spend their time?

2. What characteristics do they have?

    *   Are they confident surrounding their finances and give generously?
    *   Are they curious and open to different experiences, regularly moving out of their comfort zone?
    *   Do they perhaps stand tall and walk with confidence?
    *   How do they dress?

These are just some examples of the many emotions and characteristics that may come to mind when you think about that version of yourself. Whatever you resonate with is correct for you.

Take a few minutes now with your desire in mind to think about these questions and write down what comes to mind for you in the space below or in your own journal, if you prefer. Remember to be completely truthful with yourself, as your answers are private—for your eyes only. This process is to help empower you with this knowledge so that you can align with that version of yourself.

_____

_____

_____

_____

_____

_____

_____

_____

_____

_____

_____

_____

_____

_____

So now that you are clear on the version of yourself you wish to embody, you need to begin making shifts within the current version of yourself to align. If it is something that you are able to physically change, then make that change. For instance, if the version of yourself that has built a successful business wears smart workwear whilst working instead of casual loungewear, make that change. It will help you to get into the space to align with that version of yourself. It may seem like a simple wardrobe change, but it may actually trigger a change in mindset and allow you to become more aligned. If that version of yourself feels confidence and gratitude surrounding their finances, you could take time to look at your bank account daily. Feel gratitude for the amount of money you have with the knowledge that the Universe always supports you. Again, to reiterate, whatever resonates with you is correct for you.

You also need to do internal work to align your emotions and mindset with the version of yourself you wish to embody. Affirmations are a great technique to rewire your brain with beliefs that serve your highest good and help you to align.

For example:

1. I am confident surrounding my finances and trust that money always flows my way.
2. I am grateful to live in my dream home.
3. I am open to new experiences and I often move out of my comfort zone.
4. I feel empowered by my ability to create my reality.

Personally, I like to listen to affirmations whilst I sleep at night and have found this to be effective. You can also write them out in your journal or speak them aloud to yourself if you prefer. I would suggest using affirmations daily, as repetition is key. Using the emotions and characteristics you wrote down earlier in this stage, you can create your own affirmations or find suitable ones online. Write down these affirmations in the space below or in your own journal, if you prefer.

_____

_____

_____

_____

_____

_____

_____

_____

_____

_____

_____

_____

_____

Another technique that you can use is hypnosis. As well as hypnosis with a trained hypnotherapist, self-hypnosis recordings are a great way to access your subconscious mind from home and alter your subconscious beliefs. Day in the life journaling is another great technique whereby you script your day from the perspective of the version of yourself already living the life of your desires. This allows you to align with the high frequency emotions that this version of yourself feels.

Tools to assist you to align:

- Chapter 5: Frequency, Energy & Emotions
- Chapter 6: Affirmations
- Chapter 14: Meditation & Mudras
- Chapter 15: Journaling
- Chapter 17: Hypnosis

Goals

The second stage is to identify your goals and really get clear on them. Take your initial thought about what is it you desire to manifest, and get really clear on the details. Remember, if you are not clear with yourself about what you desire, how can you expect the Universe to be clear on what to deliver?

The importance of providing clarity surrounding your desires was highlighted during a reading I had last year. Although I began clear on what I desired, at some point, I changed my mind, and it became unclear to myself and the Universe as to what I was calling in. My original clear goal was just around the corner to manifest into my physical reality, so becoming unclear stopped this in its tracks. It is completely fine to change your mind about your desires, but you must ensure that you come back to the goal setting stage and re-evaluate what you desire so that you can provide clarity to the Universe.

Use your intuition to sense whether you prefer your goals to have lots of specific details, to give the Universe options and be surprised with the outcome, or perhaps somewhere in between. I, for example, love getting into all the nitty-gritty of the details; the more specific I get, the more excited I become about the outcome. Whereas Yvette loves to give the Universe options, and would become bogged down if she had to give lots of specific details. It is important to note that regardless of the level of specificity you prefer to have for your goals, clarity surrounding your desires is key.

How do you identify and form your goals?

I like to write my goals in present tense, as if I have already manifested them into my reality. Start by writing down the basis of what you desire to manifest, such as a new home, a loving partner or financial abundance. Then make a bullet point list of all the specific details that naturally come to mind if you prefer specificity, the core details leaving options for the Universe if you prefer to be less specific, or a bit of both if that's what you intuitively prefer. Then use the bullet point list to write your goal in the present tense. If you desire to manifest a new home, for example, the process for specific and general goals may look as follows:

Specific goal

- Five-bedroom detached house
- A large kitchen with an island
- A small grass garden
- Valued at £500,000
- Located in Newark
- A drive with space to park two cars

I live in a five-bedroom detached house in Newark, with a large kitchen that has an island which looks out onto a lovely, small grass garden. The house is valued at £500,000 and has a drive with space to park two cars.

General goal

- A minimum of a four-bedroom house
- Light, airy and spacious
- Valued between £450,000 and £500,000
- Secure off street car parking
- Close to shops and a park

I live in a house with at least four bedrooms. It is a short walk to the town centre and close to a park. The house is light, airy and spacious, it is valued between £450,000 - £500,000 and has secure off street car parking.

As you can see, both the specific and general goals make clear what they desire to be delivered by the Universe. The specific goal is calling in a very specific home, whereas the general goal is calling in a home with the openness for the Universe to deliver that or something better. Once you have formed your clear goal, you can use tools such as vision boards to give a visual representation of your goal that you see daily. You can also use your social media to follow accounts that inspire you with posts relating to your goal.

Take a few minutes now to think about the details of your desire and write these down as bullet points in the space below or in your own journal, if you prefer. Then use these bullet points to form your clear goal.

Tools to assist you with your goals:

- Chapter 7: Vision Board
- Chapter 8: Subliminal Programming

Intention

After you have identified your goals, it is time to set your intention. Setting your intention for your desires is so incredibly important. The process of intention setting involves stating what you intend to manifest with the belief that it has already happened. It allows you to place your attention and focus on your desires, give direction to your energy, and send your intention out to the Universe. Your intention that your goal has manifested into your physical reality.

How do you set your intention?

Take a moment to close your eyes, take a few deep breaths and relax. Focus on your goal for a few moments and visualise it as manifested into your physical reality. Then speaking out loud or in your mind, state, "I intend that my goal has manifested into my physical reality". Give thanks that it has manifested.

There are various ways I like to enhance this intention setting process. I often put meditation music on and meditate to help my mind relax, focus and visualise as I set my intention. I hold a crystal that I feel drawn to whilst I meditate to program it with my intention and then carry this crystal around with me afterwards. I also love to have a ceremonial cacao, particularly on a new moon, stirring my intention into the drink before consuming it. Another way to set your intention is by using a glass of water. Water is programmable, and you can program it with your intentions before you drink it. Hold the glass of water in your hands, visualise your goals and direct the energy of your intention into the water, and then drink it. Not only is this a great way to set your intention for your goals, but it is also great practice to set your intentions for your day as part of a morning routine. Remember that the process of intention setting gives your energy direction, so setting your intention in the morning sets the tone of your day.

In addition to setting your intention in the morning, I also find setting your intention before you go to sleep to be really helpful. I once went through a period of time where I would regularly wake in the night. I was sending this intention out to the Universe without even realising it. Then, one day, I felt the need to set my intention of a good night's sleep before bed, and of course, that is what I experienced.

Once you have sent your intention out to the Universe, look out for signs and synchronicities to take inspired action towards the manifestation of your desires. This could be anything from seeing angel numbers on a clock or number plate, to seeing a sign that you have asked for such as an object or animal. One of my favourite signs to ask for is a turtle, as this is something that I do not regularly see day-to-day. You can also set your intention to receive guidance from your guides or higher self, ensuring that you give yourself space to receive this guidance, such as during meditation.

Tools to assist you with intention:

- Chapter 11: Inspired Action, Signs & Synchronicities
- Chapter 14: Meditation & Mudras
- Chapter 16: Moon Phases & Ceremonies
- Chapter 18: Spiritual Protection
- Chapter 19: Discerning Positive Energies

Abundance

Now that you have set your intention for your goal, you need to feel an abundance of high frequency emotions surrounding it. Think about the emotions that you wrote down in stage one of The Nine Code of Fidelity[a]. Perhaps it was peace, joy, freedom or gratitude. Write them down below or in your own journal, and add any more that come to mind.

_____

_____

_____

_____

_____

_____

_____

_____

_____

_____

_____

There are many things you can do to help you feel these emotions surrounding your goal in the present moment. These actions will assist in raising your frequency to align you with the frequency of your goal. As per the Law of Vibration, this will help to bring your goal into your reality. Start by feeling these high frequency emotions for aspects of your life now. This then attracts more situations involving these emotions. Below are some examples of ways to raise your frequency and feel these high frequency emotions. Do whichever you feel you resonate with. Some of these tools will be covered in more detail in their own chapters later in this book.

- **Meditation:** There are so many brilliant meditations that assist you in feeling certain emotions and help you to stay present in the moment.
- **Feel love:** Use visualisation to visualise someone you love and really feel that expansion of love in your heart chakra.
- **Listen to feel good music:** Make a playlist full of songs that make you feel all the high frequency emotions. Dance and sing to your heart's desire. Feel those emotions. You can also make a playlist of songs that remind you of your goal and make you feel grateful whilst you listen.
- **Give:** This may be giving money to someone in need, giving your time to help someone, or giving someone a compliment to make their day. Everything that you give is returned to you multiplied.
- **Ground in nature:** Take a few moments to reconnect with Gaia and feel an abundance of gratitude, love and peace.
- **Journaling:** Gratitude journaling is a great way to feel gratitude for aspects of your life now and your goal. We will expand upon this in stage seven of The Nine Code of Fidelity.

It is also important to be mindful of what you watch on TV and who you follow on social media. If you are watching a programme that is low frequency, you may take on these low frequency emotions. The key here is that if you wish to watch a programme that has low frequency scenes, particularly ones that make the viewer feel how the character is feeling, you need to remind yourself that those emotions are not yours, and you do not accept them as such. In terms of social media, you should only follow accounts you resonate with. If you are predominantly vibrating at a high frequency, you will likely not resonate with accounts that provide low frequency content.

Tools to assist you with abundance:

- Chapter 5: Frequency, Energy & Emotions
- Chapter 8: Subliminal Programming
- Chapter 12: Gratitude
- Chapter 13: Grounding
- Chapter 14: Meditation & Mudras
- Chapter 15: Journaling

Forgive

Forgiveness is such an important part of the manifestation process, and yet it is often spoken about much less frequently than other aspects. In order to completely align with your goal, you need to forgive yourself, your ancestors and your past lives for self-limiting beliefs. The only person that you are harming by holding onto self-limiting beliefs currently in this lifetime is yourself. As such, it is actually a form of self-love to forgive.

Self-limiting beliefs are beliefs that you hold about yourself and the way you see the world around you which negatively impact you reaching your full potential. These often form in childhood and may also be present from past lives to keep us safe, as a result of what we process about the way we see the world around us.

Some common self-limiting beliefs include:

- I am too old or I am too young
- I don't have the time
- I am not good enough
- I don't have enough money
- You have to work hard to get anywhere in life
- Rich people are greedy
- I don't deserve to be loved
- People won't like the real me
- I don't deserve to be successful
- I don't have enough experience
- I can't make money doing what I love

One way of determining self-limiting beliefs is to think of any fears that come to mind surrounding your goal. Give yourself a moment to close your eyes, think about your goal and visualise or feel it. Are there any fears that come to mind when you do this? These are self-limiting beliefs.

Another way to discover your self-limiting beliefs is through what triggers you in other people around you. For example, you may have the belief that money is scarce and therefore it needs to be held onto. When you encounter someone freely spending money, you feel annoyed at them and think that they are stupid for doing so. It triggers you. If you take a moment to acknowledge this thought, you will see that it is something you reject in yourself due to a belief passed onto you by, for instance, your parents. As you delve into the reason behind this belief, you remember that as a child, you were often told "money doesn't grow on trees". Which, in turn, culminated into the belief that money is scarce and should be held onto. Having become aware of manifestation, you know that money is in fact an unlimited resource and always flows your way. In order to deal with the self-limiting belief and create a new belief that money is an unlimited resource and always flows your way, you must forgive your parents for this self-limiting belief.

Take a moment to visualise or feel your goal and write down any self-limiting beliefs that come to mind. Triggers that you may have noticed recently relating to your goal may also come to mind. Note these down as well, along with the self-limiting beliefs behind them.

_____

_____

_____

_____

_____

_____

_____

_____

_____

_____

_____

_____

_____

_____

_____

_____

_____

_____

_____

_____

_____

_____

_____

_____

_____

_____

_____

_____

Ho'oponopono is an ancient Hawaiian prayer used for forgiveness. This practice involves bringing the situation to mind and repeating the Ho'oponopono prayer with intention and feeling. The original prayer by Morrnah Nalamaku Simeona is as follows:

"Divine Creator, Father, Mother, Son as one... If I, my family, relatives and ancestors have offended you, your family, relatives and ancestors in thoughts, words, deeds, and actions from the beginning of our creation to the present, we ask your forgiveness... Let this cleanse, purify, release, cut all the negative memories, blocks, energies and vibrations, and transmute these unwanted energies to pure light... And it is done."

A simplified Ho'oponopono prayer by Dr Ihaleakala Hew Len consisting of four key phrases more commonly used today is:

"I am sorry
Please forgive me
I love you
Thank you"

I am sorry

I acknowledge the situation that I hold onto and take responsibility for not letting go. I am sorry for the way I have been thinking about you or the situation. I acknowledge that it is a lesson that I chose to learn before I came here, and that holding onto it is harmful to myself. It is important to note that this is not an admission of wrongdoing.

Please forgive me

You could be asking for forgiveness from yourself or the Universe; it doesn't matter. Please forgive me for having disregarded the Law of Divine Oneness in that we are all connected. I will no longer allow this situation to affect me.

I love you

I love you. I love myself. I love all of our imperfections. I send love to the situation and allow myself to heal.

Thank you

Thank you for the lesson that I received from this situation that served me in some way. I am now able to release it and free myself from the situation.

I once had a falling out with a close friend. Eventually, I came across a technique of writing down three things you love about the person each day. I now know this is part of the Ho'oponopono prayer by sending love to the person and situation. I let go of any outcome, whether that be the reconciliation of our friendship or not, and in doing so, I released the situation from myself. At the time, I was completely amazed to find that after the third day of doing this, I received an apology message from this friend, and we subsequently reconciliated our friendship. I can now see just how powerful forgiveness practice is and how powerful of a being I am to allow myself to forgive, and indeed you are too.

Once you have forgiven and released the self-limiting belief, you need to reframe the belief in a way that serves your highest good. In order to do this, you also have to consider how the belief serves you, how it affects you moving forward, and challenge the validity of the belief.

Take, for example, the self-limiting belief of "I am not capable of healing myself". Perhaps you gain attention from your health issues, and you discovered that, during childhood, you only got attention when you were unwell. So, you took in the information that there must be something wrong with you to gain attention, and it resulted in the formation of the self-limiting belief. However, holding onto this belief prevents you from healing and living the life free from discomfort that you desire. If you delve into the accuracy of the belief, you will see that there are many cases you can find of people healing themselves, and if they can do it, as per the Law of Divine Oneness, you can too. You must be ready and willing to let go of any benefit of the self-limiting belief in order to further progress.

You can then reframe the belief in a way that serves your highest good and use techniques such as affirmations and self-hypnosis to affirm the new belief in your subconscious. For example, the self-limiting belief "I don't deserve to be loved" can be reframed to "I am worthy of love".

Take the self-limiting beliefs that you wrote down earlier in this stage and reframe them below.

_____

_____

_____

_____

_____

_____

Tools to assist you to forgive:

- Chapter 5: Frequency, Energy & Emotions
- Chapter 6: Affirmations
- Chapter 14: Meditation & Mudras
- Chapter 15: Journaling
- Chapter 17: Hypnosis

Belief

The next stage is belief. You must hold a belief that your goal has already manifested into your reality. You believe so strongly that it has already shown up that there is no option other than it showing up. This is also known as active faith, which we discuss further in chapter 10.

An example I would like to give here is my university placement year. Around six months before we had to apply for placement opportunities, we had a lecture on different placements that past students had done. One that stuck with me was a placement in Germany. Moving forward to the following academic year, I attended some placement presentations in September, and once again, the placement in Germany piqued my interest. In fact, it was the only placement opportunity that I was interested in. I just had this inner knowing that it was the one I was supposed to do, despite, at the time, not speaking a word of German. Through the months that followed to the end of the year, my friends began to secure their placement opportunities which I was so proud of them for, whilst the placement I was manifesting had not yet been advertised. Then came my chance to apply in January, and I waited until April to find out I had been offered an interview that would take place in May. Throughout these months, I would openly talk with my family from the perspective that I would be living in Germany for my placement year. I remember a close friend of mine asked what I would do if I did not get the placement, given at this point, most of the other placement opportunities had closed. I completely understood where he was coming from, but I held the belief that I already had the placement in Germany and there was no other option. It must be said that I occasionally had momentary thoughts of doubt, but I quickly noticed these thoughts and nipped them in the bud, so to speak. I used affirmations to remind myself of the belief I held true. A week after my interview, I found out that I had been offered the placement!

It is important that you do not worry yourself if there are occasions where you are momentarily worried or doubtful about the outcome. The key here is to notice your thoughts and pay attention to where your energy is flowing, so that you can change the direction back to your belief whenever necessary. It is where your energy is flowing the majority of the time that makes the difference here. It may be in these times where a self-limiting belief comes up that either did not come up during the forgiveness stage of The Nine Code of Fidelity[a] or was not properly processed. It is important in this case to take a step back to the forgiveness stage and work through it.

In addition to the use of affirmations, I find visualisation meditation and self-hypnosis particularly useful to help with belief. Using these visualisation techniques, you can visualise your goals as manifested in your reality and really feel how it feels to experience them. This helps you to align with the frequency of your goal. I often use a guided day in the life visualisation self-hypnosis recording that Yvette created, as well as unguided meditation music that allows me to visualise any goal I would like.

Tools to assist you with belief:

- Chapter 6: Affirmations
- Chapter 10: Active Faith
- Chapter 14: Meditation & Mudras
- Chapter 17: Hypnosis

Gratitude

Start with having gratitude for all of the little things in your life, as you must be grateful for your life now to manifest more greatness into your life. Every morning I have gratitude for the birds singing outside my bedroom window, and I know that it is how I am awoken in my new home. As soon as you open your eyes in the morning, think of three things that you are grateful for and really feel into the gratitude. For instance, it could be your cosy bed, your family and your amazing health. Gratitude meditation is also a brilliant tool to help you feel gratitude.

Get your gratitude journaling on! Each day write down everything that you are grateful for on that day, and everything that you are grateful for that you are manifesting as if it has already manifested. Your subconscious mind does not know the difference between the gratitude you have for what you already have in your life and for your goal. Gratitude is gratitude. If you truly feel it, your subconscious mind believes it. I always begin with that which I am grateful for today and then flow into my goals. I have a lovely notebook as my gratitude journal, which makes me feel grateful and abundant to write in. So, I suggest finding a notebook to write in that elicits those feelings in you.

Gratitude journal entry example

- I am grateful for my amazing, loving family.
- I am grateful for the joy of a bird taking a bath in a puddle on my morning walk.
- I am grateful for the delicious food I had whilst out today.
- I am grateful that our book has helped so many people.

So, in the space below or in your own journal, if you prefer, think of at least three things that you are grateful for now and follow with your gratitude for your goals.

_____

_____

_____

_____

_____

_____

_____

_____

_____

_____

_____

_____

_____

_____

_____

_____

_____

_____

_____

Tools to assist you with gratitude:

- Chapter 5: Frequency, Energy & Emotions
- Chapter 12: Gratitude
- Chapter 14: Meditation & Mudras
- Chapter 15: Journaling

Let go

Letting go is a stage that can really take a lot of practice, and even now is something that I have to lean myself into doing. It is to do with releasing control of having to know how your goal will manifest. When you are so attached to a goal, it is so easy to think of all the possible ways that it could come into your reality and want to know exactly when it will happen. The truth is, the how has absolutely nothing to do with you—leave it to the Universe! I can tell you now, it will probably come into your reality in a way that you never even thought possible. When you let go of how the outcome will manifest, you leave it open to the wonders of the Universe to deliver it in the best way.

"Unexpected doors fly open, unexpected channels
are free, and endless avalanches of abundance are
poured out upon me, under grace in perfect ways"
– Florence Scovel Shinn

I want to give you a little story here. A couple of years ago, I decided I wanted to grow some apple trees from seeds. So, I got some apple seeds and placed them into the fridge in a container on a damp piece of kitchen roll to germinate. The process of germination up until the seeds sprouted took around three months. Even though it didn't happen immediately, I knew that it would. I had absolute faith in the fact, and I let go. I checked them every now and again to make sure their environment was correct, but for the most part, just let them be. I never had any doubt that they wouldn't germinate, even though I had no idea how they would. I didn't need to know the specifics of the process because it just is. Likewise, when I planted the sprouted seeds into soil, I knew that they would grow into plants. My point here is that, just like the apple seeds sprouting and growing into plants, you don't need to know how your goals will manifest into your reality. You don't need to know if it will come one way or another. That is not your business.

So let go! Let go of all expectations for how your goal will manifest and focus on the belief that it already has. You are cocreating your reality with the Universe. You have asked for what you desire, now allow the Universe to deliver however it sees fit in divine timing.

Meditation, self-hypnosis and affirmations are all brilliant tools to assist you in letting go. There are lots of brilliant guided meditations you can do for letting go. Whilst self-hypnosis and affirmations can be used to reprogramme your subconscious mind with affirmations such as, "I am open to limitless possibilities", and "I surrender to the wisdom of the Universe".

**Tools to assist you to
let go:**

- Chapter 6: Affirmations
- Chapter 14: Meditation & Mudras
- Chapter 17: Hypnosis

Receive

The final stage of the Nine Code of Fidelity[a] is of course to receive. In order to do so, you must be open to receiving. You might be thinking, "well of course I am!" But what message are you sending out to the Universe?

It is important to clear the space for your goal to come into your life. This applies to physical space and emotional space. One analogy I particularly like is a wardrobe full to the brim of clothes. You must first clear out items that you no longer wear before you are able to put new clothes into the wardrobe. In this way, you are making space for the new clothes to come in.

In the instance that you are manifesting a new partner, you must create space for that person in your life. Do they have a space in your bed? Or do you sleep in the middle? Is there space for them to hang clothes in your wardrobe? Is there a free shelf in the bathroom for their toiletries? If you have not made space for them in your life, you are sending a signal to the Universe that you are not really open to receiving what you desire at this time.

If you are manifesting money, clear out your purse or wallet. Take out old receipts or rubbish. Create a space that invites money. Smudge your purse or wallet to clear out any stagnant energy. Keep a citrine crystal in there, which is associated with attracting financial abundance. Think about where you are keeping your purse or wallet. If it is in a bag, is the bag clean and tidy, or is it full of clutter?

Feng shui your space. Create the best possible environment for you to bring in your goal. You can discover all about feng shui in chapter 9.

What do you need to clear and cleanse in your life to make space for your goal to manifest? Make a list of actionable steps below or in your own journal, and then follow through with these actions.

_____

_____

_____

_____

_____

_____

_____

_____

_____

_____

_____

_____

_____

_____

_____

_____

_____

_____

**Tools to assist you to
receive:**

- Chapter 9: Feng Shui
- Chapter 18: Spiritual Protection
- Chapter 19: Discerning Positive Energies

Of course, there may be tools found in this book that I haven't mentioned in any particular stage. Some tools, such as spiritual protection, can be used throughout the whole process, and should be used generally in your everyday life. By using your intuition, you can determine which tools you resonate with to use at any particular stage.

Remember, whilst The Nine Code of Fidelity[a] gives you a structure to the process of manifestation, the power to manifest your reality is already within you. It always has been and it always will be. You have that power. The Nine Code of Fidelity simply helps to reawaken and focus that power within you to manifest your desires.

5

FREQUENCY, ENERGY & EMOTIONS

Frequency (noun):
"The rate per second of a vibration constituting a
wave, either in a material (as in sound waves) or in an
electromagnetic field (as in radio waves and light)"

– Oxford Languages.

Vibration and Frequency

As previously discussed, the Law of Vibration states that atoms within everyone and everything are constantly vibrating. The speed at which these atoms vibrate determines the frequency. This is calculated as the number of cycles per second and given in hertz (Hz). It follows that the faster the vibration, the higher the frequency, as there are more cycles per second.

You have the ability to feel the atoms vibrating within your body. It's quite an incredible feeling, one that you will certainly know when you feel it for the first time. All you have to do is focus your intention on raising your frequency. If you have ever attempted astral projection, you will know what I mean. When you begin the process of leaving your physical body, you have to raise your frequency in order to access the astral plane. You set your intention on astral projecting, and the atoms in your body begin to vibrate faster. The best way that I can describe this feeling is as a tingling sensation, almost like pins and needles, but notably different. You feel this all over your body; an intense feeling of vibration. You can tell you have raised your frequency as you feel your atoms vibrating faster. I also find that I can often feel the atoms of my third eye charka vibrating when I am practicing meditation and focusing my intention on seeing through my third eye.

Just like the atoms in your body, everything in the universe is made up of energy. It follows that emotions are energy and have an impact on your overall frequency and health. Emotions may be of a higher or lower frequency, which can be deciphered by how the emotion feels in your body. If feeling the emotion makes you feel constricted and heavy, then it is a lower frequency emotion. Whereas, if the emotion makes you feel expansive and light, then it is a higher frequency emotion. There are tools that can be used to determine the specific frequency of particular emotions. However, I feel that the best tool you can use is your intuition, whilst noticing the feeling the emotion gives in your body. You know if you are feeling low frequency. Perhaps you feel anger or frustration when triggered by something. You can literally feel the emotion in your physical body. Likewise, you know if you are feeling high frequency. Perhaps you feel an abundance of love or a sense of joy for the life you have created for yourself.

Feel and Process Low Frequency Emotions

If you do experience low frequency emotions, and it is completely normal to do so, you must feel, process and release these emotions. It is really important that you do this deep inner healing so that you no longer let it affect your frequency and health. These could be emotions such as anger, jealousy, fear or envy, to give just a few examples. If you suppress these low frequency emotions, they will just reappear in other situations in your life or manifest as health issues.

Often the emotions you need to process are felt as a result of a trigger, bringing a self-limiting belief to the surface. That is, of course, providing that you take a moment to reflect on why you were triggered to determine the self-limiting belief. The emotion can act as an anchor for the self-limiting belief in your subconscious mind.

For example, you may have just heard about the straightforward, easy birth of your friend's child. You feel triggered by this and have a sense of anger and hurt, but you don't understand why. The fact that you are triggered suggests that there is deep inner healing that needs to take place. You should go back to the root cause of the emotion and deal with it there. It may be that it originated from something in your childhood or even possibly from a past life. By allowing yourself to feel and process the situation that resulted in you first feeling the emotion, you release the emotion and allow yourself to heal. It is possible to meditate to determine the self-limiting belief behind the emotion and where this originated. You can then use the Ho'oponopono forgiveness prayer to forgive and release the situation that resulted in the low frequency emotion. Regression hypnosis is also an excellent tool for allowing your soul to take you to those memories that you are ready to heal and to see things from a different perspective. In doing so, you can forgive and release the situation and call your power back.

Many people aren't aware that with consciously creating your own reality comes deep inner healing work. Whilst it can and should be fun to create your dream life, it is also necessary for you to do this deep inner healing work. Feeling and processing emotions you have been suppressing and ignoring isn't the most light-hearted part of the creation process. However, it is so rewarding when you have done the work and released the low frequency emotion you have held onto for so long. You feel so much lighter. You are no longer triggered by things that once triggered you because you have processed the emotion at its root. It allows you to really awaken your power by removing these limits you have placed on yourself. Remember that this is an ongoing process, and as emotions arise, they should be felt and processed.

How To Raise Your Frequency

Energy can neither be created nor destroyed but rather transmuted. As per the Law of Perpetual Transmutation of Energy, we are able to change our frequency if we so desire. Everyone may feel low frequency at some point or another, so don't feel as though you have to be high frequency all the time. Having said that, you attract that which you are a vibrational match to. Whilst it isn't a problem to occasionally feel low frequency, it becomes a problem when you are constantly in a state of low frequency. You will begin to attract things and situations that you are a vibrational match to in that low frequency state. So, if you find yourself feeling low frequency, do things that help you to raise your frequency to stay aligned with your desires to bring them into your physical reality.

There are various ways that you can raise your frequency to bring what you desire into your reality. One technique that I use is to listen to music of a specific frequency. Insight Timer is a fabulous app for this. You can simply search, for example, health frequency, and you will be able to play music to that frequency. Frequencies that I constantly find myself listening to are the frequencies of gratitude and abundance, especially whilst I am journaling. There is frequency music for everything. As everything is energy, everything has its own specific frequency. Whether it be health, wealth or love, listening to frequency music whilst you sleep is an effortless way for the music to permeate your subconscious mind. You don't even need to take time out of your day as it allows your subconscious mind to do the work whilst you sleep.

I also find that going out for a walk and reconnecting with nature is a great way to raise your frequency. Being present whilst you walk and listening to all of the noises around you will certainly help you to feel grounded in the present moment. Moving your body through other means, such as yoga, can be beneficial in raising your frequency too.

If you enjoy music, listen to some feel-good, energetic music. By dancing around to the music and singing along, you will instantly feel energized and uplifted. I would also recommend pairing music with something else that you enjoy doing, such as cooking or baking.

Have you ever found that just being around animals raises your frequency and you feel better within yourself? We visited the Farm Animal Sanctuary in Evesham, United Kingdom, and were surrounded by rescued animals that we were able to spend time with. It was a great experience and one that I would highly recommend. Being around animals is always a great way to raise your frequency. I am sure at some point in your life you have heard the purr of a cat. When cats are happy, they purr. The purr, which of course has a specific frequency, has substantial healing benefits.

Ensure that you are listening to your body and giving yourself time for self-care. Allow yourself to be alone in your own company to reset and discharge the energy of others. This could be by having a relaxing bath, followed by a meditation. The most important thing about what you choose to do to raise your frequency is that you actually enjoy doing it.

Being in Energetic Alignment

Since everything in the universe is energy, it is of the utmost importance that you are aligned energetically with regard to your future self and the things you are manifesting into your life. You won't be able to attract things into your life with which you aren't aligned. Energy, and thus frequency, are magnetic. Have you ever noticed that when you're feeling aligned and like the best version of yourself, that people reach out to you? This works the same way with absolutely anything that you are manifesting; vibrate at the right frequency and attract it into your life. It really is that simple.

"Everything is energy, and you come to earth to learn how to manipulate that...to become a master manifester"
—Dolores Cannon

You will attract an abundance of what you put out into the universe. So, it is crucial that you are putting higher frequencies out into the universe in order to attract your intentions. If your intentions come from a place of love, they will always manifest into your reality. Something that I do regularly, particularly whilst meditating, is that I envision my heart chakra as a very bright, glowing orb spinning in my chest and send love out into the universe.

Raise your frequency in any way that resonates with you and you will absolutely enhance the manifestation process. Reprogramme your subconscious mind, think better thoughts, but also spend time doing whatever it is that you love, that brings you joy, and that makes you feel like the best version of yourself. Radiate loving energy out into the universe, practice gratitude and give thanks for everything that you have in your life.

6

AFFIRMATIONS

One of the most significant things that you can do to change your reality is to repeatedly use positive affirmations on a daily basis. I cannot stress this enough; affirmations changed my life. As previously mentioned, words are spells and everything that you say or think goes straight out into the universe. Although I have always known this to be true, a reading that I had really illustrated it. There were some aspects of the reading that had only ever been thoughts in my mind. It was actually quite amazing to have the fact that your thoughts go out into the universe exemplified in such a way.

You must be careful about what you say, even in jest, as neither your subconscious mind nor the Universe has a sense of humour. It is paramount that you remember this. Always, always, always speak your truth in a positive way.

What Are Affirmations?

Affirmations are powerful statements you can use to reprogramme your subconscious mind and reframe self-limiting beliefs. You have the power to change your life through the use of affirmations; all it takes is consistency and belief. You can use affirmations for absolutely everything that you intend on manifesting into your life. There are many affirmations available that others have already created, or you can easily create your own. There are a few aspects to consider when choosing affirmations from others or making your own:

1. Affirmations should be written in the present tense as if it is already present in your physical reality.
2. Use words that indicate that your desire is already present, such as I am and I have. 'I am' is a powerful phrase as what follows is what you attract. Avoid words that imply lack, such as I want and I need.
3. Affirmations should be written in a positive, empowering manner. Ensure that they focus on what you want to create and not what you don't want. If I said to you, "don't think of a purple donkey", you automatically think of a purple donkey. The same is true for your subconscious mind if you use negatives in your affirmations. So instead of writing, for example, *I don't spend time procrastinating*, you should write, *I am productive each and every day*.
4. Affirmations should be written as concise statements.

Here are some affirmations to give you inspiration for creating your own. Of course, you are also welcome to make use of any affirmation that you resonate with.

I am strong and I support myself with ease.
I attract a wealth of abundance in every aspect of my life.
I am powerful, I am loved and I am protected.
I am empowered by my ability to create my reality.
I release all that no longer serves my highest good.
I awaken my divine power within.
I am deeply connected to my intuition.
It is safe for me to be my true authentic self.
I attract money with ease.

I am a magnet for all that serves my highest good.

I radiate confidence each and every day.

I feel complete freedom over how I choose to spend my time.

I am confident surrounding my finances and trust that money
always flows my way.

I am healthy, happy and loved.

I am open to all opportunities that serve my highest good.

I am grateful for my perfect health.

I feel safe, secure and grounded.

I am exactly where I am supposed to be.

I trust in the divine timing of the Universe.

I am divinely supported by the Universe.

I am worthy of a life full of luxury.

I am financially abundant.

I am successful in everything that I do.

I am a powerful creator of my reality.

I am surrounded by love.

I easily connect with other like-minded people.

I am enough and I love myself unconditionally.

I am open to give and receive love.

Everything that I need is within me.

I release the past and live fully in the present moment.

Reprogramme Your Subconscious Mind Using Affirmations

You have to inherently believe that you are worthy of receiving that which you desire. You can write or speak affirmations until you are blue in the face, but in order to manifest, your subconscious mind, as well as your conscious mind, has to believe them to be true. You have to reprogramme your subconscious mind and let go of any notion that you are not worthy. Because you absolutely are worthy. You are worthy of manifesting absolutely everything that you desire.

With regard to affirmations, of course it is powerful to speak them, but I have found that it is an extremely effective tool to listen to them whilst I sleep. Whilst you're asleep, your brainwave state changes and produces theta and delta waves making your subconscious mind exceptionally impressionable. This makes it the perfect time to listen to affirmations, as they will permeate your subconscious mind, making them even more effective.

There are so many affirmation videos and audio available on media platforms and apps to play whilst you sleep. These are readily available for absolutely everything, such as wealth, health and love—to name a few.

A YouTube channel that I love and recommend to you is 'Manifest by Jess'. There you will find prerecorded affirmations that are on a loop for around 8 hours, so they play to you all night long. It takes no time out of your productive day, and trust me when I say that having affirmations read to you whilst you sleep is very effective.

Some affirmations I used to listen to were for self-love, which helped tremendously. Your reality shifts and you become the best version of yourself. I also find that the affirmations for total abundance are fantastic to listen to whilst you sleep, as they cover a much wider variety of areas within your life. I am a completely different person embodying a completely different mindset since I began listening to affirmations whilst I sleep.

Another technique that I have found to be extremely effective is to write affirmations on flash cards. Make them bright and make them stand out. Then stick them to your bathroom mirror, or anywhere in your house for that matter, as long as they are somewhere that you will see them regularly. For example, as you use your bathroom every day, what better time to read the affirmations than when brushing your teeth or going about your daily beauty routine? Manifestation tools do not need to take time away from your regular schedule. After all, work smarter, not harder.

Affirmations should also be included on your vision board. Reading and speaking affirmations that coincide with your intentions will only enhance the manifestation process. Partner the picture of your new car with the words 'I am so grateful to be driving my new car', say the affirmation and feel the gratitude as though the car is already yours.

Florence Scovel Shinn wrote a book called *The game of life and how to play it*, which can be found as part of *The complete works of Florence Shinn*, and it is absolutely worth the read. In this book, she gives examples of affirmations to use for each aspect of your life. It is, in fact, these affirmations that I have written on flashcards and stuck to my mirror. She stresses the importance of the words you speak and how even speaking affirmations differently can change the outcome of the manifestation. The Universe takes what you say literally, so for example, if you assign a timeframe to the manifestation of your goal, then that is what you will get, rather than it manifesting sooner.

You may notice yourself repeatedly speaking negative affirmations such as "I am tired", and you may often do this without consciously thinking about it. Remember that you create what you repeatedly speak and believe. So by speaking negative affirmations, you are creating more of what you don't want. It is important to notice what you say so that you can consciously change your perspective to create what you actually desire.

7

Vision Board

One of the most commonly known manifestation techniques, and the one that I am certain you would have heard about, is the use of a vision board. For those of you that might not have heard of one before, a vision board is just that; a board where you put photos and affirmations representing the goals that you intend on manifesting. Quite simply put, your vision for your life. Anything that you can envision, you can have. It is actually that simple. You might include a photo of a house, a car or even a specific holiday. In fact, as we write this book, an image of the front cover is on all three of our vision boards.

Your vision board should be placed somewhere you can see it every day. It is important for your mind to see these images and envision them as already being part of your life. I personally have both a physical and an electronic version of my vision board. In a world where technology is always evolving, you absolutely should use this to your advantage wherever possible.

Physical Vision Board

A physical version of a vision board is always great to do because it allows you to spend time choosing photos, printing and cutting them out, and physically arranging them on your board. Whilst doing this, you are able to consider what emotions the version of yourself feels that has already manifested each of your desires, and really feel and embody these. For instance, feeling gratitude as if you already have those things in your life. The things you include on your vision board don't necessarily have to be materialistic; you can include other things like affirmations such as 'I am grateful', 'I am blessed' and 'I am abundant'.

Virtual Vision Board

A great way to create a virtual version of your vision board is on the Hay House app, Canva or on other similar websites and apps. The virtual version of my vision board has been created as a phone wallpaper. How much time do you spend on your phone each day clicking from app to app? You always have your phone on you, but you're not always at home and able to gaze upon your physical vision board. Alexa also has hers as her desktop wallpaper on her laptop. The same images and affirmations that are on my physical vision board are on my virtual version, but generally, it is much more convenient and less time-consuming to update your virtual vision board. Similarly to the process of making a physical vision board, making a virtual vision board also allows you to consider which emotions to embody to align with the version of yourself that has already manifested your desires.

Vision boards are personal, so I'm not saying you have to have it as your lock screen for everyone to see. Instead, by having your vision board on your home screen, you get a glimpse of it each time you open your phone. Again, when you are automatically scrolling through your phone, these images will be etched into your subconscious mind, and you will begin to effortlessly manifest that which is on your vision board. It is even possible to create your own wallpaper on your fitness watch, so it is a great idea to have your vision board on your watch for you to glance at each time you check the time.

Creating and Updating Your Vision Board

Be creative when making your vision board. Order business cards with your new job title or business, edit a first-class plane ticket to have your name on it, print a blank cheque and write it out to yourself with a figure you wish to manifest, or even photoshop yourself onto the tropical beach of your dream holiday destination. You can use your goals that you set out in the goal setting stage of The Nine Code of Fidelity[a] to help you choose what to put on your vision board. In setting your goals, you intuitively felt the level of detail you prefer to give concerning your desires. If, for your dream home, you like to be really specific and your goal includes a kitchen with an island, include that on your vision board. Whereas, if you like to be less specific and your goal includes a light, airy and spacious home environment, then find a photo that represents this for you for your vision board. Be as specific or as general with the items that you choose for your vision board as resonates with you. The most important thing is that whatever you choose, you feel the emotions that the version of yourself feels, having already manifested your desires.

Do absolutely everything you can to make your vision board unique, make it you, and make it stand out! If you're making a physical vision board, use glitter, bright pens and stickers, and make yourself feel great about your life when you look at it. Do anything you can to make sure you feel gratitude and excitement about your life when you see it. After all, gratitude is the source of all abundance. The more that you feel grateful for—and beautiful soul—you have everything to be grateful for, the more reasons the Universe will give you to be grateful.

A vision board should be updated regularly, as when your goals come to fruition, you will remove the images and swap them for new ones. We are constantly manifesting and evolving as human beings, and our vision boards should reflect this. It's rather interesting to see how quickly things manifest each time you update your vision board. Creating and updating a virtual version can be much more time efficient, especially when we live such productive lives. It doesn't take long to search for images and save them to your phone. You can even do this whilst having a nice relaxing bath, during your daily commute if you aren't driving, of course, or even whilst you have your lunch at work.

How To Create a Vision Board

1. Do something to ensure that your vibration is high and aligns with that of your desires—this is imperative. Put on some music, sing, dance, meditate. Do whatever you resonate with to uplift your vibrational energy.
2. Find yourself a board. This can either be a physical one (a pin board or a photo frame, both work wonders) or a virtual board on an app.
3. Choose photos online or in magazines that relate to the desires you wish to manifest. These photos should resonate with you and elicit the emotions within you now that the version of yourself feels having manifested them.
4. Print and cut them out if you are making a physical vision board. If you are creating a virtual vision board, import them to the place where you are creating it. Look at the photos that you have chosen and envision them as part of your life.
5. Arrange them on the board in a way that resonates with you—get creative!

6. Feel all the emotions and excitement that you have in the knowing that what is on the board is already yours.
7. Give thanks. Give thanks that all of your desires have already manifested themselves into your life.

To give you some prompts for your vision board, focus on some of the following category ideas:

- Relationships
- Spiritual
- Purpose
- Hobbies
- Personal Growth

- Financial
- Recreation
- Business
- Home
- Health

Which areas do you feel drawn to?

Once you've finished your vision board, if it's a physical one, position it somewhere in your house where you will see it frequently. If you have made a virtual version, which I do encourage, make it your phone, laptop, computer or tablet background. Nothing is saying that you have to do one or the other. Why not create a physical version and a virtual version? The more you can glance at your vision board, the better, and the faster the items included on your vision board will manifest themselves into your life.

My advice to you would be to put on some high vibrational music, make sure that your frequency matches the lifestyle you wish to embody through your vision board and begin to create, create, create! Make it artistic, make it unique, and most importantly, feel the exact emotions you would feel if it was already in your life. Feel the excitement and give thanks. Gratitude is so important, and I cannot stress that enough. Give thanks as though it is already yours, and so it is.

8

SUBLIMINAL PROGRAMMING

You are constantly being influenced by every single thing in your environment, whether you are aware of it or not. Your conscious mind only uses approximately 5% of your brain power to process the things you are consciously aware of. Your subconscious mind is responsible for using the remaining approximately 95% of brain power to process things you are not consciously aware of. It is in your subconscious mind that your beliefs about yourself and the way you see the world are formed and stored. These beliefs ultimately influence the way you consciously act.

Your subconscious mind is constantly processing everything that it is exposed to. It ultimately wants to keep you alive and safe. So, it stores programs pertaining to your experiences and forms beliefs based on these experiences.

When you are scrolling through social media, watching TV or listening to music, you are particularly susceptible to programming. You can choose whether or not you wish to use this knowledge to your advantage. All three of these modalities can be used to enhance the process of creating your desires if you use them with such an intention.

Social Media

Have you ever heard that you become like the top five people you spend most of your time around? You take on their personality attributes; successful people surround themselves with even more successful people. We are constantly learning and evolving as human beings, and who we surround ourselves with can have an astronomical effect.

The same applies to those you surround yourself with on social media. Your subconscious mind is like a sponge, especially when you spend hours upon hours mindlessly scrolling through your social media feed. Your brainwave state changes making you even more susceptible to subliminal programming. When you're scrolling through social media, your brain is on autopilot, like when you're driving home using the same route you do every day, and you realise you can't remember a huge chunk of your journey. Your brain is in a trance-like state, and you have to be so careful about what you expose yourself to on a daily basis. Have you ever noticed when you're scrolling through videos and reels that the songs used get stuck in your mind for hours upon end? Your mind is impressionable.

You can, and you absolutely should use this to your advantage. This is such a great manifestation tool with technology evolving so quickly and it being such a big part of our everyday lives. It is with the utmost importance that you only follow accounts that resonate with the life you are creating. If you desire a life that involves travelling, then follow travel accounts. See the stunning photos of the bright blue ocean and the golden sands grace your feed. Envision yourself there. If you want to live a healthier lifestyle and have the body you have always wanted, follow the fitness accounts and embody that lifestyle. The term 'social media influencer' has the word influence right there in the name. You are being influenced by everything that you expose your mind to, whether you are aware of it or not.

By filling your social media feed with content that you envision for your future self, you are subconsciously programming your own mind. If you are going to spend even a fraction of your day scrolling through social media, then you must use this to your advantage. Some of the best accounts you can follow are positivity and mindset accounts. You click onto your social media, and there's a quote waiting to tell you how amazing and powerful you are.

Cookies on social media track the content that you follow and interact with the most to enable them to show you more and more similar content. This is designed specifically so that you spend more time using their social media platform. If you're going to spend longer scrolling through your social media feed, then it is for your highest good to ensure the posts that you expose both your conscious and subconscious mind to are positive, and resonate with the version of yourself that you wish to embody.

I cannot stress this enough, unfollow accounts and people that do not bring you the joy and satisfaction that you desire in your life. If someone is constantly complaining or posting low vibrational content that doesn't resonate with you, unfollow them. It really is that simple. You wouldn't surround yourself with these people in real life because if you did, then you would feel your energy change in a negative way. So don't follow them online either. By continuing to follow accounts like those, you are hindering your own manifestation process and are pushing the life you wish to embody further away. As I mentioned before, your mind goes into a trance-like state, and information flows into your subconscious mind. This is perfect for manifesting if you use this tool to your benefit, but other people's negativity is absolutely not what you want to manifest.

The best thing that I have learnt in the past year, which is something that has changed my mindset in the best way possible, is that the way that someone responds to a situation is a reflection of themselves and has absolutely nothing to do with you. So don't worry about offending that person you went to school with ten years ago. If they have a problem with you setting clear boundaries, then that is a reflection of them, not you. If you no longer resonate with them or the content that they provide online, unfollow them.

The same applies to brands that you follow on social media. Does the content resonate with the version of yourself that you are embodying? You might be rather fond of their products, but if the content that they are providing doesn't resonate with you, unfollow them. That doesn't mean that you can't still purchase their products. It just means that you aren't exposing your mind to content you don't resonate with. Follow brands that incorporate the lifestyle you envision for yourself, whether it is cars, property, travelling or fashion. Follow manifestation, mindset and coaching accounts that provide positive affirmations, messages and helpful information for you to see on a daily basis. Use social media to your advantage.

The accounts and content you expose yourself to on a daily basis through any means of social media make all the difference to your life. Follow accounts that make you feel great about yourself, that make you feel empowered and like the mighty beautiful soul that you are. You are essentially using social media as a vision board to programme your subconscious mind with your desires. It is important to note that social media can often be very curated, and you should treat it as such.

Whilst social media can be a great tool to aid your creation process, it is important to give yourself a set amount of time to spend on social media. This means that you will use this time more wisely, and you won't spend countless hours mindlessly scrolling for the sake of it. You will appreciate seeing the content that you have ensured aligns with your desires. By having a set amount of time for social media, you make sure that you are actually being present in your life and appreciating it now.

Music

Music has a huge part to play in our day to day lives. I certainly listen to music every single day, and I'm sure you do too. Have you ever actually stopped and thought about the lyrics that you're singing? Those very lyrics are being etched into your subconscious mind. Those very catchy heartbreak songs that you sing on repeat whilst driving to work, even though you aren't heartbroken in the present moment, could be attributing to the future you. Not so long ago, I had a catchy song called *Dirty Little Secret* playing on repeat, and do you know what happened? I ended up with just that, a dirty little secret, which was well manifested if you ask me. But that's all we're saying on that matter, swiftly moving on.

Songs are created to be catchy and get stuck in your head, so you play them over and over. How many times have you had a song stuck in your head, and you hear it everywhere? That is exactly how manifestation works. You have been effortlessly manifesting without even realising it. You can't stop thinking about that song, and then you get in the car, and it's playing on the radio, then you walk into the supermarket, and there it is playing again. The next time you have a song on repeat because of its catchy tune, I urge you to take a moment to stop and listen to the lyrics that you are singing.

Words are spells. This means you literally speak your truth. Do you remember the word you would say when performing magic tricks as a child? The very word 'abracadabra' translates as I will create as I speak. When you're in a sad mood, and thus in a lower vibrational state, you tend to gravitate towards the low vibrational sad songs. Why? Because you're vibrating at that frequency. In reality, all it does is keep you within that lower vibrational state, and you feel worse for it. The best thing you can do is to put on some happy, positive, upbeat music that you can dance around to, and do exactly that—dance! You'll be surprised how quickly your mood and frequency changes, and being in a higher vibrational state is key for manifesting positivity into your life.

Recently I have been listening to some of the songs I used to listen to when I was younger. Whilst the tunes are catchy and make you want to get up and dance, I honestly cannot believe some of the lyrics. These are lyrics that we sang as children and teenagers but never really took note of or fully understood. Music plays a huge part in our day to day lives and in shaping the minds of the younger generations. Your subconscious mind is even more programmable when you are younger, and it is paramount that you do understand the lyrics that you are exposing yourself to. By repeatedly singing particular song lyrics, you are inadvertently creating the situation written about in the song in your physical reality.

I'm just going to go slightly off track for a moment, but I promise it's relevant. Back in 2020, I did an angel card reading. I drew myself four cards, and one of them said to dance with life and do something to change my energy. I really resonated with that at the time. I was not in the same headspace that I am in now, and I needed that to change. Music became a big outlet for me. I would put in my headphones with some music on and dance. I would dance like no one was watching (and thankfully, they weren't), and it changed my energy. I felt so much better for it, and I still do the same thing now. So, dance with life, dance with every possible opportunity and feel the music. Feel your energy change and get yourself into alignment with your dreams and intentions. This is a sure-fire way to accelerate the manifestation process. Just bear in mind, as previously mentioned, it is important that you make sure that the lyrics are relevant to what you are manifesting.

I am not by any means saying that my playlist is perfect, but I do constantly reassess whether or not the songs that I am listening to resonate with the version of myself that I wish to embody. The songs that I add to the playlist solely depend on my mood and frequency at the time, so sometimes, I need to remove songs that I know contain lyrics that I do not want to manifest.

Each tune attributes a different frequency in hertz, so even if you feel the lyrics resonate with you, the frequency in which the tune is made could actually be hindering rather than helping your manifestation process. However, it is important that, as always, you use your intuition. You may feel that you embody a higher vibrational state when singing a song, regardless of the frequency. As a powerful being, you, of course, have the power to override the hindrance and still accelerate the manifestation process.

Intentionally Using Music for Manifestation

Music can be absolutely incredible for manifesting so many different things. By intentionally choosing the music you listen to, you can use it to assist in aligning with the version of yourself that you wish to embody. I found myself listening to a lot of music which expresses self-confidence and self-worth within the lyrics. This helped tremendously when manifesting a better sense of self-worth and self-love. Have you heard the saying "fake it until you make it"? These songs project a sense of confidence, and if you act confident for long enough, you become confident. Who's really going to know that you were faking it at the beginning? After a while, even you don't know you're faking it anymore, and it becomes who you are.

There are also plenty of songs out there that have affirmations as lyrics. These lyrics are absolutely beneficial to reprogramme your subconscious mind. Some of these, of course, are on my playlist. Did you hear the song that was circulating all over social media called *I am* by Baby Tate, Slide Da Monster and Flo Milli?

The lyrics say, "I am healthy, I am wealthy, I am rich...". Every time I had a negative thought, such as I am tired, drained, or any other word with negative connotations, I would quickly revert to singing these lyrics. I am is, of course, a powerful phrase, and by telling myself that I was tired, I was only going to make myself even more tired.

Another song that I listen to is called *Energy Mantra – Remix* by Michael Seven. This is another one that you might have heard on social media. It is a great song to sing during your morning commute or even in the shower. The lyrics are as follows, "Everything that I need, I already have. Everything that I have, is all that I need. Anything I desire, I will receive. Because my reality is created by me". Sing your truth, you beautiful soul, because you can have anything that you desire.

There are so many songs out there that you are sure to discover one that will benefit any area of your life. There are songs containing health affirmations that allow you to sing good health into existence at every given opportunity. I invite you to search for these songs on the internet to really get a feel for their catchy tunes. I can assure you that you will constantly be singing them too. If you have a song stuck in your head, it might as well be catchy affirmations that will assist you for your highest good. Mantras and songs activate a wider proportion of our brains than just simply speaking alone. This is what makes affirmations that we are able to sing so much more powerful. The catchy tune will stick in your brain, and you will find yourself singing the affirmations on a regular basis.

Making Music Personal

Although there are so many songs available that incorporate affirmations, why not make your own? Make it personal to you with your own catchy tune in order to make your affirmations stick in your subconscious mind. This can be as simple as using one affirmation that you resonate with and singing it in a way that is catchy to you. It doesn't need to be complicated, and you certainly don't need any special equipment to do so. I once found myself singing the affirmation, "I am strong, and I support myself with ease". I actually wrote down this affirmation for my cactus that needed a little extra support to stand up straight. It wasn't long before I found myself singing it whilst dancing around the kitchen. It was really catchy, and I felt my frequency rise as I sang it. This exemplifies how music can be personal and interpreted differently depending on the listener. The intention behind this affirmation for my cactus was to be able to support itself physically. Whilst for me, it was to be able to support myself financially. I also received a mantra during meditation one day that goes, "I am healthy, I am wealthy, I am divine. I receive what I want in perfect time". It is catchy, and I find myself singing it all the time. You can, of course, record yourself singing, along with you clicking or clapping along with the tune, and create an actual audio that you can listen back to whenever you feel like it. You can make the process as simple or as technical as you like.

Another great way to use music in a personal way is to create a playlist of songs that you associate with your desires being present in your physical reality. For instance, I have a playlist of songs that I associate with driving around in my new car. When I listen to this playlist, I instantly visualise being sat in my car. I hear the song that I am listening to as if it is playing in the car, and this really helps me to visualise the experience. I can literally feel myself there. I can feel the seat under my body, the features in the car, and I can sense the person there with me. I feel a huge sense of gratitude that this car is mine. By listening to this playlist, it allows me to easily visualise, and since the subconscious mind doesn't know the difference between something real and visualised, it helps to bring it into my reality even faster.

TV, Streaming and Media

For many people, watching television programmes is a big part of their day-to-day lives. Television programmes do just that; they programme your mind. In this day and age, this includes the streaming of media on various platforms. Some people get up in the morning, and the first thing that they do is turn on the news. Whilst you might feel as though it is beneficial to know what is going on in the world, you are only shown what the mainstream media companies want you to see. The majority of the time, what is shown on the news is negative and used in a way to keep you in a state of fear. Fear is a low frequency emotion. If you choose to repeatedly focus your attention on fear-based programmes, you will become an energetic match to fear and create situations that exemplify this in your life. That is not to say that I am completely unaware of what is happening in the world. I choose to educate myself on current situations from other outlets where the primary objective is not to spread fear. I can then use my intuition to determine whether or not the information given resonates with me. Rather than beginning my day with fear-based programmes, I prefer to spend my time meditating, journaling and grounding in nature. Give it a try if you're prone to start your day by watching the TV, and see if you can feel a shift in your frequency.

Whether you believe it to be true or not, your subconscious mind is easily programmable by absolutely everything around you. Whether you are consciously sitting watching the TV or whether a programme is playing in the background. Your mind is impressionable, and anything that you watch on TV plays a role in shaping your future self. When watching TV, your brainwave state changes, making your mind even more susceptible to programming. So the next time you think about watching that reality TV show with all the drama, think about whether or not that is something you wish to be part of your reality. Instead, be selective and make a conscious effort to choose a TV show that resonates with the person you are aligning with. You can tell that your mind is impressionable when a catchy song comes on the TV, and you find yourself humming or singing along to the tune for the rest of the day.

I am always very selective about the programmes that I watch, and generally, I don't watch mainstream TV. I watch prerecorded shows, which eliminates any adverts. Adverts are clever. They are specifically designed to make an impression on your subconscious mind. It may be so that you purchase the product in the advert, or even develop the reason for needing it. Think about it, how many times have you watched an advert for a product to cure an itch, for example, and you find yourself feeling the need to scratch? People get paid a lot of money to create these adverts; they know exactly how to get the information into your mind in such a short timeframe. They know how to create an effective advert, and the aim of the game, of course, is for you to buy the product, regardless of what it might be.

If you do watch something on TV, then make sure that it is for your highest good, even if it is just playing in the background. Watch things with the view of nourishing your mind and soul rather than watching pointless shows to pass the time. Watch things that will only enhance your capabilities. Watch shows about the things you are manifesting—about travelling, investments and other areas of your life you would like to develop. Watch videos that show other people's experiences of what you desire to help you to visualise them in your life.

You should surround yourself with and only expose your mind to the things that resonate with your desires in any area of your life. Quite simply put, if nothing changes, then nothing changes. If you continue to go about the same routine day in, day out, then all that will manifest is more of the same. You can't heal in the same environment that made you sick. Make the changes and make the changes now. Change what you are exposing your mind to. It is time for you to take responsibility for your actions and for your life.

If you have time in an evening to sit and binge-watch a series, and we've all been there and done that, then perhaps a better option is to pick up a book or listen to an audio recording or podcast. Think about what it is that you're about to watch. Be selective about what you allow into your mind. Use your time well, and invest it in yourself. The future version of you will absolutely thank the present you for it.

9

Feng Shui

Feng shui is an ancient system that uses ancient knowledge and wisdom handed down by generations to create a feeling of harmony and flow within your environment. It allows energy to come into the home, bringing in positive high frequency energy known as chi or lifeforce. When chi is stagnant, it can cause energetic problems within that area. This can then have a negative impact on the bioenergetic field of those in the home who enter that area. As per the Law of Vibration, if the energy or chi in that area is low, then it's a vibrational match to low frequency energies or entities.

Using this ancient Chinese method of feng shui, it is possible to ensure that the chi or energy flows freely and easily throughout the home. This will raise the energy and frequency of the chi higher to a more auspicious level. We use a special Chinese map or grid called a Bagua as a tool in feng shui. When the Bagua is placed upon a property or room, it is possible to see which zone pertains to which area of one's life.

Wealth & Prosperity	Fame & Reputation	Love, Relationships & Marriage
Colour: Purple Element: Wood Number: Four	Colour: Red Element: Fire Number: Nine	Colour: Pink, Red & White Element: Earth Number: Two
Family & Health Colour: Green Element: Wood Number: Three	**Centre & Health** Colour: Yellow, Orange & Earth Tones Element: Earth Number: Five	**Children & Creativity** Colour: White Element: Soft Metal Number: Seven
Knowledge & Personal Growth Colour: Blue, Green & Black Element: Earth Number: Eight	**Career** Colour: Black & Blue Element: Water Number: One	**Helpful People & Travel** Colour: White, Grey & Black Element: Metal Number: Six

MAIN DOOR

Figure 2. Feng shui Bagua.

How to Use a Bagua

Remember, firstly, that when you use the Bagua, it's more of a diagnostic tool to ascertain why certain areas of your life are holding low or stagnant energy and how you can enhance and improve the flow of energy in that area. It may be quite easy to see and rectify the problem when you view the areas of the Bagua through a different lens.

To begin with, draw a Bagua on a piece of transparent plastic sheet and place the Bagua over a two-dimensional drawing of your home. There are several variations of feng shui, some of which use a compass, but I prefer to keep it as simple as possible. So, instead of using a compass, I simply align the bottom of the Bagua with the front door. This means that the career area is in line with the front door. The door that you use most of the time is what I would consider your front door, even if it is technically your back door. The door where energy enters and exits your home is the one that you want here. Again, there are versions of feng shui which state it must be the main door as the house was built. I've found that using the door that we use all of the time works exceptionally well for us.

If the building is not square, then I have found elongating the Bagua or stretching it out works very well. This is providing that there are nine squares on the board, and you can see which area of the building pertains to which area on the map.

As you look at the Bagua over the building and see the relevant sections of your life, it is possible to use the tools of feng shui to ensure the energy is flowing beautifully and that the energy is of a high frequency.

You should declutter all areas of your home regularly as, if there is clutter, it is very easy for the chi energy to stagnate. When you hoard or hold onto things, you are really telling the Universe that you have lack as you don't want to let anything go. This makes it harder for the energy to flow in and out. I find having a good declutter every three or four months is exactly what is needed to keep the energy free flowing.

The Bagua map is an excellent tool to identify areas within your home which may be affecting your physical and emotional health. When using this tool to assess your home, work with what you already have. There is no need to rush out and buy shiny new objects that have attributes of a particular area. The chances are that you already have all that you need to enhance the life force or the chi in your home. It just may be that it is currently in the wrong room, but that is easily remedied when you begin to consider the feng shui of your space. There is an abundance of information available to remedy each area of your home, and it would not be possible to cover everything here.

So, we will look at a few easy, simple remedies for each area of your home.

Career

The career area is positioned at the front centre of the Bagua and benefits from the number one and the colours black and blue. This doesn't mean that you need to paint your walls this colour, but you can incorporate an element of the colour into the area. It may be that you purchase a new front door or paint it so that you have a black or dark blue door to enhance the water element. As this area is associated with the water element, you should avoid having too much of the earth element here. Earth is destructive to water as it absorbs it, and it is characterised by aspects such as rock and stone. The squiggle shape often used to represent water is helpful here too. Perhaps, if your key is in the door, place a beautiful tourmaline keychain on it. The black tourmaline represents the colour of water, and is also very effective at cleansing the energy of anyone who enters your home. Be conscious of what you hang on the wall in this area. Is it a painting of the sea, a boat, a river or a waterfall? Or have you inadvertently placed a photograph of a calming pile of stones or rocks that may be better placed elsewhere?

You may find that most of the areas on the Bagua map overlap rooms, and in our home, the career area goes from the hallway into the cloakroom. To enhance the career area here, we've placed a large black water pitcher and utilised it as an umbrella stand. As the walls in this room are an earthy tone, the black pitcher allows us to bring in the element of water without redecorating the walls in the space. You have got to work with what you have, and perhaps you love the earthy tone of the walls in that area. In this case, you can use accessories to bring in the particular element associated with the area.

Helpful People and Travel

The area to the right of the career area is the area for helpful people and travel. The colours that benefit the flow of energy in this area are white, grey and black. The element associated with this area is metal, and the number associated with this area is the number six. The shape that benefits and enhances this area is an oval shape. If you want to increase the number of helpful people within your life, or you wish to travel to the most beautiful or influential places, then take a look at this area of your home. Ensure that the energy is flowing, and see how you can enhance this area with the associated colours, element and number.

Knowledge and Personal Growth

To the left of the career area is the area of knowledge and personal growth. The colours associated with this area are blue, green and black, and the element is earth. Here, as well as incorporating the colours, the number eight and the square shape are beneficial. It may be helpful to add a book shelf with an array of interesting books. I also love to have a healthy plant in this area that symbolises the tree of knowledge and my own personal growth. It is important that you take care of and nurture the plant.

Family and Core Health

Behind the knowledge and personal growth area is the family and core health area. It is enhanced by the colour green and the element of wood. This element is enhanced by water, but metal should be avoided as this leads to a destructive cycle. I love to place photographs of family here, and you may also choose to place a luscious green plant that is very well cared for. The number three and the rectangular shape also benefit this area.

Centre and Health

The centre or middle of the home is the health area. This area benefits from yellow, orange and earth tones. The number five and the element of earth are also beneficial. This area is enhanced by fire, but you should avoid wood. Always ensure this area is tidy and free from clutter, as it is energetically symbolic of your health and that of your family. A tiger's eye crystal placed in this area to protect the home is also a good option to consider. It is in the centre of the house where I stand to give gratitude and thanks to our home for the protection and warmth that it provides us.

Children and Creativity

To the right of the health area is the area for children and creativity. This area is enhanced by the colour white and the soft metal element. It is associated with autumn, the circle shape and the number seven. You may choose to place photographs of your children and grandchildren or creative pieces that have been made in this area.

Love, Relationships and Marriage

Behind this area, towards the back right hand side of the Bagua, is the love, relationships and marriage area. If you want to inject passion into your love, marriage and relationships, then this is the area to focus on. Add a splash of pink, red or white and remove all clutter. The number two can be used to enhance this area. Ornaments and pictures should be in twos, never singular, unless you're trying to tell the Universe that you are single. Ensuring that the energy flows and that there are always two of something in that area is really important. For instance, it could be a photograph with two gorgeous birds or a happy photo of you and your partner. The shape associated with this area is a square. If you have plants in this area, ensure that they are very well tended to, as this is the growth of your relationship.

Fame and Reputation

In the middle, at the top of the Bagua, we have the fame and reputation area. The colour to amplify the energy here is red, but you could also use orange as it signifies flames. If you want to fan the flames as it were, add some wood in this area. The wood will support and amplify the fire and, in turn, your recognition and fame. You could also use the number nine here to amplify that fire energy. For example, having nine peacock feathers in a vase signifies the air to fan the flames. It's better to avoid the water element where possible here, which can be attributed to blues and blacks. Logically, water dampens down fire, and we do not want that in this area. The shape that is associated with this area is the triangle.

Wealth and Prosperity

Left of the fame and reputation area is the wealth and prosperity area. This area is all about increasing your prosperity. It is enhanced by the colour purple, and holds the element of wood. The element of water is good to have here, but you would want to avoid metal where possible. The number associated with this area is four, and the shape it resonates with is a rectangle. Placing beautiful pieces of citrine in this area will really benefit you financially.

Making Changes with Feng Shui

A few simple changes using the tools of feng shui can make a real difference. For example, if you desire to have a partner in your life, have you made space for their clothes in your wardrobe? Do you have two bedside tables? What images are you surrounding yourself with in your home? Are there two items together or just singular items? These are all subliminal messages that could be keeping you in a life of singledom. Make space in your wardrobe for their clothes, and ultimately send a message to the Universe that you are ready for a partner.

When thinking about abundance and prosperity, does it feel like the energy of money could flow freely throughout your home? Is your wardrobe crammed with clothes that you don't wear but are hanging onto just in case? What sort of message is that sending to the Universe? If you have clothes in your wardrobe that you haven't worn in years, consider which area this affects. Is this creating stagnant energy in your relationship zone or your prosperity zone? Go through your wardrobe and sort out the contents. Give anything you haven't worn in the last year to charity. Equally, give anything that doesn't make you feel great to charity. Someone will really benefit from those clothes. The more you give away, the more you will receive energetically. As you take each piece of clothing and connect to it, if it makes you feel good, then keep it. If you are uncertain, then that too goes in the charity pile. You need to free up the flow of energy, and hanging onto old things doesn't allow that energy to flow.

Remember, the Bagua is a simple tool to identify possible problem areas so you can easily rectify them to raise the frequency and energy in that area. Having good high frequency music on in the home, the type that makes you sing and dance, is always wonderful and will instantly raise the frequency and vibration.

10

ACTIVE FAITH

One of the most important aspects of manifestation is active faith. Well, let's face it, every aspect of manifestation is important, but you have to have faith. You have to believe because that is how manifestation works. Believe that it is already yours and it will be. In fact, it already is. Have no doubt in your mind that you already possess it, and it is already yours. You have to embody the version of yourself that already has what you are manifesting before it comes into fruition. What is that version of yourself like? How do they act? Believe that you are worthy, and you will receive.

Trust in the Universe. Trust that anything that you desire, you will receive. You are a limitless being with limitless potential. You co-create your reality with the Universe, and you will always receive what you have asked for or something even better.

It might sometimes seem difficult to keep the faith, especially when you can't yet see your desired outcome in your physical reality. Rest assured that your desires are on their way. Remember that absolutely anything in your life coming to an end is simply making room for something new, something even better, and for your desires to manifest themselves into your life. There is a brilliant story about a bamboo tree that perfectly encapsulates having active faith. The bamboo tree takes five years to grow out of the soil from a seed. Every day the tree was watered and nurtured by a gardener, despite no visible progress of growth. In the fifth year of watering, the seed sprouted, and the bamboo tree rapidly became 80 feet tall. The moral of the story is that if the gardener had stopped watering the tree because he saw no progress year on year, he would not have seen the fruits of his labour. He held active faith and never doubted that, one day, he would see the bamboo tree.

Active faith can mean buying a keyring for your new house or car keys or a new suitcase for that trip you are manifesting. Take steps to show the Universe that you trust the process, that you have active faith, and you will receive that which you desire.

It is important to make room for your desires to manifest. Are you manifesting a new pair of shoes? Clear out your wardrobe, give away any shoes you no longer wear and make room for them. On multiple occasions, both Alexa and I have cleared out our wardrobes and given clothes that we no longer wear to charity. Within a few days we both won a competition for a substantial voucher to spend at one of our favourite clothing companies. This has happened on multiple occasions.

Another example of active faith is when I was around twelve years old; so we're throwing it back a good few years now. Justin Bieber was my idol; we're talking playing songs on repeat on my iPod and posters all over my bedroom walls. I just absolutely knew that I needed to see him in concert. The time had come, and Justin Bieber was finally in the UK! He was due to sing at the Capital FM Summertime Ball. I wanted to go; I needed to go. However, at the time, my parents said no because it was on a Sunday night in London. Despite this, I just had this inner knowing that I was going to the concert. I didn't know how because it was in London and I was twelve. I didn't actually have a job to buy the tickets or the transport to get to London, but I had every faith that I was going. It wasn't even a question. A few days later, Trent FM announced a competition, and the prize was… tickets to the Summertime Ball. Of course, I had to enter. I texted the number to enter the competition and headed to my Great Grandma's house for a family gathering. I remember the day well. It was a beautiful summer's day, and we were all laughing and having a great time in the garden. My phone rang. I ran inside with eager anticipation, and it was Trent FM. I had won the tickets! I screamed with joy at the top of my lungs; I did it. I was going to the concert! I won two tickets, one for me, and one for my mum. Just you wait, beautiful soul, it gets even better.

It was at this point, of course, that Alexa knew that if I was going, then she too needed to go to the concert. Again, with active faith, she knew she was going and trusted the process, even though she didn't know how. The next day, the same competition was announced on the radio. So, she texted the number to enter the competition, and we headed out for the day with the family. I remember this day well too. We were at our local Abbey Park; the sun was shining, we had a picnic, and we had been paddling in a stream that ran through the park. As I recall, it was a very high vibrational day, full of laughter, family and nature. To say that the phone signal there at the time was limited is an understatement. When it was time for the winner to be announced, we were pacing around the gardens, moving the phone high and low, ensuring that the phone had signal for the much-anticipated phone call; the phone call we undoubtedly knew was going to arrive. The phone rang, but this time as it was the final competition, multiple people had been selected to be the potential winner. The competition had been run across the Capital Network, and there were four people on the line but only one winner. We were eagerly awaiting for Alexa's name to be shouted out, and then it happened, Alexa was the winner! She had won another two tickets! There was absolutely no doubt in her mind that she was going to the concert, and she too had manifested the tickets. Absolutely everyone we tell this story to is amazed that we both won. Usually, knowing someone that has won a competition on the radio is unheard of. But two sisters winning within two days. Wow. Our manifesting skills and active faith were on point. We were very much aligned with the version of ourselves that were to attend the concert, and we had faith that we were going.

We have been aware of and practicing manifestation for many years now, but this is one of the first recollections we have of manifesting something so big, so quickly and simultaneously. Generally, we do tend to manifest very well together, we bounce off each other's energies, and it absolutely works in our favour.

Surrender to the manifestation process. The Universe always has your back. It is not your job to worry about how things will manifest and come to fruition into your life. Just know that they absolutely will manifest in divine timing. Have faith. Have faith you beautiful soul. You are powerful, and you are capable of manifesting absolutely anything that you desire.

11

INSPIRED ACTION, SIGNS & SYNCHRONICITIES

An astronomical part of the manifestation process is inspired action. Inspired action is about taking steps towards your goal because you feel intuitive drawn to. The Universe will prompt you at every given opportunity to push you in the right direction. The direction of your dreams and desires. This may be through receiving various signs and synchronicities that allow the Universe to communicate with you. In fact, at various stages throughout writing this book, we received signs and synchronicities and took inspired action that prompted us to write content previously not considered.

It is imperative that you follow your intuition and take inspired action. The Universe will guide you as much as possible, but you have to take steps to become the version of yourself that you are aligning with. Take the inspired action, take the leap of faith and embody the attributes that the future version of yourself already wholeheartedly possesses.

Many years ago, I asked the Universe if it was definitely the correct path for me to become a midwife at that point in my life. I had three young children, and going to university would be a huge change that I had to be certain about. Literally two minutes after I asked for guidance, the postman knocked at the door and gave me the mail. I quickly opened the mail, and the

British Journal of Midwifery fell open onto the floor. As I picked it up on the page it fell open on, I saw a double page spread with the title *spiritual midwifery*. I felt that this was a sign from the Universe in response to my question. So, I took inspired action and drove to college to collect my reference for my university application. En route, I started to question the validity of the previous sign from the Universe. I pulled into the car park across the road from the college, and as I went to get a car parking ticket, a huge gold car drove into the car park. A tall, baldheaded older gentleman got out of the car, walked towards the ticket machine and began speaking to me about cars. We were walking in the same direction and continued the general conversation. At the point we departed ways, he put his hand on my arm, looked straight at me with angelic blue eyes, and kindly said, "you are going to make the most amazing midwife". This man didn't know me prior to this interaction, and didn't know that I was considering an application for midwifery. I quickly crossed the road, turned back to wave goodbye, and he had completely disappeared into thin air. If that wasn't a sign from the Universe, then I don't know what is. Remember that you can always ask the Universe for guidance, and you will always receive an answer if you are open to it.

When you are in alignment, you will notice signs and synchronicities around you more and more frequently. You may see these as numbers, such as on a clock, a number plate or the odometer in your car. You can also ask for a specific sign, such as an object, an animal, or even receive guidance through a song on the radio. You will intuitively know when you receive divine guidance in the form of signs and synchronicities. How often have you noticed numbers such as 111, 444 or 888? The Universe is speaking to you. Listen. Each different number sequence embodies a different set of meanings. It is important to consider what you were thinking about the second before you saw the number sequence. The meaning of the number sequence can vary depending on what this is, and what you intuitively feel it means for your particular situation. There are many number sequences that you may repeatedly see as signs and synchronicities. We have provided our interpretation of the meaning of some of the number sequences that we see most often. We have used gematria, which is a numerology system that gives a numerical value to a word or phrase, to further support the meaning.

Number	Meaning	Gematria
111	Your intentions are being amplified... you are manifesting quickly.	Magnified.
222	Focus. Commit to your desires.	Commit.
333	You are being guided through whatever it is that you are focusing on. What is meant for you, will always find its way to you.	Meant to be. Angelic host.
444	You are one with the Divine. You are capable of creating a life that you love.	I am the chosen one. Earth Goddess.
555	You are worthy of all your desires.	I think, therefore I am.

666	Your intentions are in good hands, you are completely supported by The Universe.	My name is God.
777	Good things are coming...luck is by your side.	Good good good good good good good. Lucky light.
888	Abundance at its finest, trust the divine plan.	Divine plan.
999	Listen carefully, the Universe is communicating with you.	Listen carefully.
000	New beginnings, huge changes are coming.	-

Table 1. Interpretation of the meaning of number sequences.

During the process of writing *The Power of Three*, when we hadn't written anything in a little while, we would all start to repeatedly see 999. We were being nudged to finish something, and we all knew this related to the book. The Universe was giving us the nudge that we needed to finish this book. We wholeheartedly knew that you, you beautiful soul, were waiting in eager anticipation to read our book, and that we were writing this book to pass on our knowledge, to change so many lives for the better.

On another occasion, throughout the writing process, we all received a synchronistic email from Hay House—a large publishing house. The subject of the email read, "It's Back! Your opportunity to get published". We, of course, all read the email describing a writer's workshop full of tips and tricks and an opportunity to be published by Hay House without an agent. We then, however, continued to live our productive day-to-day lives, and the email was pushed to the back of our minds. Until another email arrived. This time, the subject read, "Do you dream of being an author?"—another nudge from the Universe. We absolutely knew that we needed to take part in the writer's workshop and submit our manuscript. We needed to take inspired action. The Universe made the course financially accessible, and despite the event being in a different time zone, we booked the course. The whole week of the writer's workshop, we all repeatedly saw 333. This illustrated that we were being guided through what we were focusing on.

Ask the Universe for signs. Trust the synchronicities that you are shown, and trust your intuition. You will know when you are following the right path—trust me when I say you will feel it. Everything will flow so effortlessly for you.

12

GRATITUDE

Gratitude absolutely is the source of all abundance, and I cannot stress this enough. The more you appreciate and give thanks for things in your life, the more that will flow into your life effortlessly. One of the techniques that I use on a daily basis is gratitude journaling. Every morning, right before I eat my breakfast, I take five minutes out of my day and write in a notepad the things that I am grateful for. These are a mixture of things currently in my life, as well as things that I am manifesting. This is a great way to speak your desires into existence. Your subconscious mind doesn't know whether these things are your current reality or not, so giving thanks as though you already possess them accelerates the manifestation process. Not only that, but by consciously thinking about the things you are grateful for, your whole outlook on life changes. The little things don't bother you anymore because you have so much to be grateful for.

Another technique I use as soon as I open my eyes in the morning is that I put my hands on my heart to connect with my heart energy, and I say three things that I am grateful for, and I really feel the gratitude. Let's circle back to the fact that words are spells and that you create as you speak. I am is the most powerful phrase that you can use. Saying "I am grateful for..." every morning is the best way to start your day. Just saying three things you are grateful for before you start your day puts you in the best mindset, and you find that positivity and abundance flow effortlessly.

If you constantly think about what you don't have and how much you really want something, then you cause a sense of lack. By causing a sense of lack, you are essentially telling the Universe that you don't have it, and you will push it further and further out of reach. This is why it is so important to give thanks and gratitude for the things that you do have and even for the things that you are manifesting as though you already possess them.

I am so grateful every single day for everything in my life, whether it be a blessing or a lesson. Every day that you wake up, you have a choice. You have a choice to be bitter and frustrated, or you have a choice to feel gratitude for the things in your life. You have to take accountability because only you can change the way your mind views the world, and the way you view the world makes all the difference.

Gratitude is everything. If you change your mindset, you can, and you will change your life. Absolutely everyone has something that they can be grateful for. Every day that you wake up breathing the air into your perfect lungs and get to see and hear the beauty that is Mother Earth Gaia, you have something to be grateful for. The more you give thanks, the more the Universe will give you reasons to be thankful.

There are guided gratitude meditations available that help you feel grateful for all aspects of your life. They don't have to take up a huge proportion of your day. By choosing a five-or-ten-minute morning meditation, you can set your day up in the best way possible. You can also do visualisation meditations to visualise your goals, and feel the gratitude that you have as if they are manifested in your life.

Right now, I invite you to stop and pause for a moment and write down three things you are grateful for, either using the space below or in your own journal, if you prefer.

• _____

• _____

• _____

Make this part of your daily routine, and don't get too fixated on having to write three things. Of course, you can write more than three, but make it a daily practice to remind yourself and the Universe of all the reasons you have to be grateful.

I constantly have moments when I just stop for a minute and reflect on how much gratitude I have for my life, and it makes my heart feel so full. You often don't realise, but you're currently living the life that the past version of you once dreamt about. Appreciate where you are right now and how far you've come rather than simply where you're headed. Enjoy the journey that is your life, and give thanks for every single moment.

13

GROUNDING

A manifestation tool we have found to be particularly beneficial is that of grounding. Grounding is the process whereby you connect your energies with that of Mother Earth Gaia. From a scientific perspective, grounding outside allows the positive ions in your body to pass through your feet into the Earth. These are exchanged for negative ions that your body resonates with. This process helps you to feel grounded in your physical body, which is important because you chose to be here on Earth in a physical body at this time. It also helps you feel more connected with the energies of the planet and Divine Oneness. By being grounded, you have a heightened perception of your senses. You may notice the birds singing, the leaves rustling, or the scent of the flowers to a heightened degree. You can also ground whilst you focus on your goal and send your intention out to the Universe. We have found this to be a brilliant way to accelerate the manifestation of our desires. Everything in the universe is energy. Once you learn how to manipulate the universal energy in your favour, you can have absolutely anything you desire.

Grounding is such an incredible way to raise your frequency and assists you in becoming a vibrational match to that in which you are manifesting. You feel so much better when you have been outside and connected to nature, and the better you feel, the easier and quicker it is for you to manifest. It really is that simple.

There are multiple ways in which you can ground, but to simply put it, take off your shoes and your socks, and walk barefoot on the grass, in a stream, or even through the mud; the latter, of course, is to please your inner child. You can ground on any surface that even mildly conducts electricity and connects you to the Earth.

We are most fortunate to live in the countryside, where we are surrounded by nature. Everywhere you turn, there is another field, another forestry or another footpath just waiting to be explored. We are also blessed to live close by to multiple country parks and Abbeys with stunning grounds to walk around. Generally, and more so when the weather is nice when we are out and about exploring, we take off our shoes and socks and walk barefoot for a while over the fields. I invite you to do the same, and you will feel your energy shift. If you are not in an area where you feel comfortable doing this, and you have a garden at home, then you can definitely stand and ground at home in your garden.

To further enhance the grounding process, I had a bracelet made of petrified wood beads. My intention was to use the bracelet to connect myself to the Earth element, even when I was not outside and amongst nature. By my skin being exposed to the elements of the Earth, the bracelet would then help me to stay grounded and thus enhance the manifestation process. You can also use grounding shoes, such as Earth Runners, that allow you to ground whenever you leave your home whilst wearing the sandals. I have found both of these tools to be very effective ways to enhance the grounding process.

Another tool I use to enhance the grounding process is to visualise myself grounding whilst meditating. A great way to do this is to visualise roots coming out the bottom of your feet like a tree. Visualise the roots winding through the Earth, through various levels of sand and rock, and eventually wrapping themselves around a gorgeous, glowing crystal in the centre of the Earth. The energy from Mother Earth Gaia can then flow through your roots and through your crown chakra, and your intentions and energies can start to flow both ways.

Again, grounding is a great way to connect your energy with that of Mother Earth Gaia, and the more connected you are to the Universe, the easier you will find it to manifest your dreams and desires.

14

MEDITATION & MUDRAS

Meditation is such an amazing practice to centre yourself and bring your awareness back to the present moment. Whilst there are many different types and purposes for meditation, they are all rooted in bringing your attention back to the present moment. Often in life, we are on the go so much that we forget to live in the present moment.

Contrary to popular belief, meditation practice is not the absence of thoughts but rather acknowledging the thoughts that come without judgement, and letting them pass by. This allows us to stay in the present moment; without being fixated on thoughts about the past or future.

There are so many different types of meditation, and I find it can often become a little overwhelming when choosing which meditation technique to practice. The key here is that any type or amount of meditation is better than doing none at all. It is also important to set your intention for your meditation practice. Perhaps it is an intention to be focused, to be relaxed, to cleanse your chakras, or to receive information that serves your highest good. Whatever it is, make sure you set this intention before you begin your practice to give the meditation direction.

Guided vs. Unguided Meditation

The first stage in choosing your meditation practice is whether you would like it to be guided or unguided. There is no right or wrong decision here; it really comes down to your own personal preference. I use both depending on the meditation technique I wish to practice. Insight Timer, which I have been using for years, is my go-to place for both guided meditations and meditation music for unguided meditation.

Guided Meditation

When you are first learning to meditate or using a new type of meditation, guided meditation can be really helpful as a teacher guides you through the meditation. This can help you to keep your focus and awareness on the meditation. Therefore, it is particularly helpful if your mind is prone to wandering or racing, as there is a voice to focus on to keep your awareness in the present. Guided meditation can be practiced using a guided meditation audio at home or in a group class in person. There is an abundance of guided meditations out there with a huge variety of teachers and topics, so you would certainly find ones to suit you.

Guided meditation can be useful when building strong fundamentals and confidence in your practice. The support you receive from being guided in your practice helps to reassure you that you are doing it correctly. It can also be used to enhance your visualisation abilities as you will often be prompted to visualise certain things, such as the colour blue of the throat chakra during a chakra meditation. By starting with guided meditations to enhance your visualisation abilities, you can then use these abilities during unguided meditation to visualise the goals you desire to manifest.

Unguided Meditation

Unguided meditation is, as it sounds, practiced without a meditation teacher guiding you through the meditation. You may choose to do unguided meditation whilst listening to meditation music that is just music without a guide speaking, or you may choose to do it in silence. It is usually practiced individually, but we often do group meditations to meditation music on new moons when setting our intentions for our goals.

Unguided meditation can be used to visualise a goal you desire to manifest as you can decide what to focus on during the meditation. In this respect, you have more freedom with the ability to customise your meditation. You can also lead yourself through the stages of a guided meditation that you have used before in your head. This allows you to be undisturbed by a teacher's voice.

Meditation Posture

It is important to find a position for meditation where you feel comfortable and relaxed whilst your mind remains alert. There are various postures you can take to meditate including, the following four postures; sitting, lying down, standing and walking. Regardless of the posture you choose to take, there are some main points you should bear in mind:

- A straight back and spine to promote the flow of energy
- Shoulders dropped down and relaxed
- Chin slightly tucked under
- Jaw relaxed
- Hands rested as per the posture or in a mudra position (more on these later in this chapter)

Sitting

There are various sitting positions you can take including: variations of sitting cross-legged on the floor (quarter, half and full lotus), kneeling on the floor, sitting with your back against a wall, and sitting in a chair. Whichever sitting position you choose, the key is to be comfortable. If you are in any discomfort at all, you will be more focused on that than the meditation practice.

Personally, my favourite sitting position is on a chair, as it provides the perfect amount of support for me to remain comfortable for the entire meditation practice. The chair sitting position consists of sitting on a chair with your spine straight, feet flat on the floor, and hands resting in your lap, with your palms facing up.

Lying Down

The lying down posture is known as savasana or corpse pose in yoga. It can be particularly helpful if you aren't able to take a sitting position for extended periods due to discomfort. I love meditating lay down, especially first thing in the morning. I find it to be a great, comfortable position to be in for an entire meditation. It is, however, important to ensure you remain alert enough to stay awake and not drift off to sleep. Unless, of course, you are practicing sleep meditation.

You can do whichever type of meditation practice you like lying down. For example, body scans, sound bath meditation and sleep meditation all work particularly well with this posture.

Savasana consists of lying down on your back, with your feet hip-width apart. Your feet should be angled outwards slightly, and your arms rested down either side of your body, with your palms facing upwards. If you find this uncomfortable, you can have your knees bent with your feet flat. You can either do this posture on the floor or on your bed—it's your personal preference. It will likely depend on the type of mediation you are practicing as to which you choose. For some meditations, such as sleep meditation, where the purpose is to eventually drift off to sleep, practicing it in your bed would be perfect.

Standing

If you are familiar with practices such as Qigong, you will be familiar with standing meditation. The standing posture is brilliant to help you feel grounded during your meditation practice. It is also great to do if you find it uncomfortable to take a sitting posture or you fall asleep lying down.

One type of standing meditation is Zhan Zhuang, which means standing like a tree. To practice Zhan Zhuang, you begin in the initial position known as Wu Chi. You should begin by standing with your feet shoulder-width apart and your toes spread. Your spine should be straight so that you are standing tall, and your shoulders should be relaxed. Slightly and naturally, bend your knees and roll your hips forward. Allow your arms to naturally hang at the sides of your body at a distance as if you have a small ball under your armpit, and face your palms inwards towards your body. Slightly tuck under your chin, relax your jaw and place your tongue on the roof of your mouth. Keep your eyes open with a soft gaze. Start by doing this posture for one or two minutes a day and build it up over time. From this starting position, there are numerous variations of the standing posture you can practice. For instance, with your palms facing you, you can either raise your arms in front of your chest as if you are holding a big balloon or raise your arms in front of your stomach as if you are holding a small balloon.

Walking

Walking meditation is a type of mindfulness practice that involves paying attention to the world around you whilst also being aware of the physical sensations in the body and the way in which you hold yourself and move. There are many types of walking meditation that you can practice, and it can be done in any environment, from a walk in nature to a walk through a busy street. It is a great way to improve your mental clarity and awareness. More often than not, when walking alone, you are placing your attention on something other than the walk itself. This may be looking at your phone, listening to music or being lost in your own thoughts. Walking meditation brings your mind and body connection back into alignment.

During one type of walking meditation, you keep your eyes open and use the rhythm of your steps to bring you back to the present moment if your mind starts to drift. Begin standing still, take a deep breath and focus your awareness on how your body feels. Sense what your posture is like and how the ground feels beneath your feet. As you start to walk, pay attention to the rhythm of your steps as if it were your breath during sitting meditation. Now take a moment to scan your body for any areas of tension and release them. Observe what is happening in the world around you; what can you smell, hear and feel? Perhaps the birds are singing, or you can feel a cool breeze against your skin. How do these physical sensations make you feel? Focusing once again on your body, notice the length of your stride and the pace at which you are walking. If your mind begins to drift, bring your awareness back to the rhythm of your steps. Repeat this process throughout your walk, bringing your attention from your body to the environment and back again. Initially, you may feel self-conscious when consciously observing your posture and how you walk, but this is simply about observing, and you will become more comfortable with it the more you practice.

Types of Meditation

There are so many different types of meditation, including the following examples:

- Chakra meditation
- Mantra meditation
- Body scan meditation
- Visualisation meditation
- Sound bath meditation
- Binaural beats meditation
- Gratitude meditation

As there are various types of meditation, do whichever you feel you resonate with at the time you wish to mediate. So, if on one day you feel you resonate most with practicing a body scan, do that, and if on another day you feel you resonate most with practicing a chakra meditation, then do that. Below we will discuss two types of meditation; chakra meditation and mantra meditation.

Chakra Meditation

The purpose of chakra meditation practice is to clear and align your chakras. The term chakra originated from the Vedas text in ancient India. Chakra (*cakra*) is a Sanskrit word that translates to wheel and is used to refer to the wheels of a chariot in ancient texts. It is believed that the knowledge surrounding chakras was passed down through oral teachings for many years before it became written in the Vedas, so the exact date of origin of chakras is unclear.

Chakras are energy centres of the body where *prana* or life force energy concentrates. Chakras can be likened to spinning wheels of energy. These energy centres are positioned both in and around your physical body, including above your head and below your feet. There are many chakras which form various chakra systems consisting of differing numbers of chakras such as five, seven, ten and twelve. Chakras may be major or minor energy centres, and although they aren't physically visible, they can be felt and visualised. For instance, there are minor chakras on your hands which I feel when meditating and doing energy work as a whirl of energy in my palms. I also often feel a tingling sensation around my major chakras, such as my third eye chakra and my crown chakra.

The Seven Chakra System

The most common chakra system in the Western world today is the seven chakra system that runs down your spine. This originated from the work of Swami Purnananda in 1577 and was further introduced to the Western world in 1919 through the translation and commentary of ancient texts by Sir John Woodroffe in *The Serpent Power*. Traditional texts associate the chakras with mantras, symbols, elements and deities. However, in 1977, Christopher Hills made the association between the seven chakras and light frequencies corresponding to the colours of the rainbow. This work is outlined in the book *Nuclear Evolution: Discovery of the Rainbow Body*. This is the colour system of the seven chakra system we commonly see today. In addition to the association with colour, each chakra is also associated with a different location and properties.

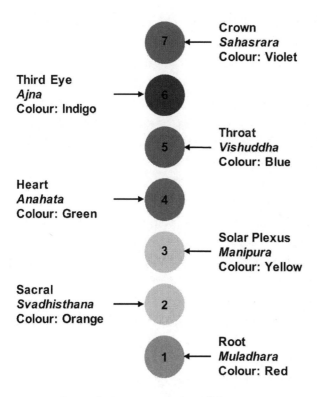

Crown
Sahasrara
Colour: Violet

Third Eye
Ajna
Colour: Indigo

Throat
Vishuddha
Colour: Blue

Heart
Anahata
Colour: Green

Solar Plexus
Manipura
Colour: Yellow

Sacral
Svadhisthana
Colour: Orange

Root
Muladhara
Colour: Red

Figure 3. A representation of the seven
chakra system of the human body.

The first chakra of the seven chakra system is the root chakra (*Muladhara* in Sanskrit). It is located at the base of the spine and vibrates at a frequency pertaining to the colour red. It is the chakra of aspects such as survival, stability, security, and physical identity. It is responsible for our sense of feeling grounded. When the root chakra is blocked and out of alignment, it can lead to feelings including that of being stuck, stagnant, powerless and disconnected.

The second chakra is the sacral chakra (*Svadhisthana* in Sanskrit). It is located just below the navel in the lower abdomen and vibrates at a frequency pertaining to the colour orange. It is the chakra of aspects such as passion, creativity and sensuality.

When the sacral chakra is blocked and out of alignment, it can lead to a lack of creativity, depression and obsessive behaviour. The third chakra is the solar plexus (*Manipura* in Sanskrit). It is located above the navel in the upper abdomen and vibrates at a frequency pertaining to the colour yellow. It is the chakra of aspects such as motivation, confidence, power and a sense of purpose. When the solar plexus is blocked and out of alignment, it can lead to feelings of low self-esteem and control issues.

The fourth chakra is the heart chakra (*Anahata* in Sanskrit). It is located in the centre of the chest area and vibrates at a frequency pertaining to the colour green. It is the chakra of aspects such as love, trust and relationships. When the heart chakra is blocked and out of alignment, it can lead to relationship difficulties, insecurity and loneliness.

The fifth chakra is the throat chakra (*Vishuddha* in Sanskrit). It is located in the throat area and vibrates at a frequency pertaining to the colour blue. It is the chakra of aspects such as clear communication. When the throat chakra is blocked and out of alignment, it can lead to anxiety around communication and feelings of shyness.

The sixth chakra is the third eye chakra (*Ajna* in Sanskrit). It is located in the centre of the forehead and vibrates at a frequency pertaining to the colour indigo. It is the chakra of aspects such as intuition, imagination and foresight. When the third eye chakra is blocked and out of alignment, it can lead to a lack of clarity and direction.

The seventh chakra is the crown chakra (*Sahasrara* in Sanskrit). It is located at the very top of the head and vibrates at a frequency pertaining to the colour violet. It is the chakra of aspects such as divine connection, enlightenment, and a state of higher consciousness. When the crown chakra is blocked and out of alignment, it can lead to a disconnect with spirituality and a closed mind.

Mantra Meditation

Mantra meditation is a form of meditation that involves chanting, singing or silently repeating in your mind, a word or phrase. I first learnt about mantra meditation years ago through the book *Chant and be Happy: The Power of Mantra Meditation*, based on the teachings of A.C. Bhaktivedanta Swami Prabhupāda. This book was handed to me by a man one day as I was walking through the city centre; synchronicity at its finest. The mantra meditation that I learnt through this book is the Hare Krishna mantra, and it is one that we all use on a regular basis.

Hare Krishna, Hare Krishna,
Krishna Krishna, Hare Hare
Hare Rama, Hare Rama,
Rama Rama, Hare Hare
[Pronunciation: Huh-ray – Krish-na – Rahm-uh]

According to the ancient text of the Vedas that originated in ancient India, Krishna is the foremost God who oversees the demigods that are seen as administrators to the universal affairs. God has many names, and Krishna is one name of God. In the Hare Krishna mantra, Krishna and Rama address God, and Hare addresses the energy of God. The chanting of this mantra produces transcendental sound vibrations, raising your frequency and reviving the pure Krishna consciousness within. By calling upon Krishna to assist with your desires, they will manifest themselves at an accelerated rate.

The beauty of the Hare Krishna mantra and mantra meditation is that they can be practiced anywhere. Perhaps you have some time whilst you're driving, cooking, in the shower, or at work—the options are limitless.

Mudras

A hand mudra is a physical hand gesture that has a specific energy behind a powerful meaning. It has an energy signature of an intent that has been used for thousands of years. This energy signature or intent has the power to affect you psychologically and spiritually when you focus upon it for a period of time. The word mudra, which is a Sanskrit word, can be translated as to bring forth enchantment. These hand gestures are truly empowering and so easy to connect with and use intuitively and discretely anywhere.

You are most likely using mudras in your everyday life without even thinking about it. We might see a child clench their fist when they are angry or fold their arms across their solar plexus when they feel uncomfortable or cross. For some, it may be placing their hands together as if to pray in a gesture of love and gratitude. Or perhaps they raise a hand when they don't want anyone to come close to them or give someone a thumbs up. Mudras are not only gestures but may be perceived as a hidden language.

The Aryan (Vedic) tribes used ritual hand positions as early as 1800 BC; we can see that through history the Sages of Ancient India used mudras in ritual and particularly within dance, enhancing the energy of the mudra even more. We often see the deities with their hands in the position of a mudra in order to emphasis the energy that they were holding and the intent behind the hand gesture within that moment. We see images of Buddha and also Jesus in Orthodox Christian art with varying mudras, which all have a specific sacred meaning.

Mudras are an amazing tool that we can focus our intention on as others have done before us. By using these ancient symbols, we are tapping into the energy of those in the collective consciousness that have used them with the same intent before.

There are thousands of mudras and some excellent books and websites with vast amounts of easily digestible information and pictures that will help you to choose the right mudra for you. There is a mudra for each of the chakras, and they can be used whilst meditating to release energy from the chakras that no longer serves you and to realign and calibrate the chakras into harmony. There are also mudras for each organ in the body or to release or gain a certain emotion or to assist the body in healing and transformation from disease.

There are a few mudras that I love to use personally, and I'll share them with you here. Firstly, the mudra for balancing all five elements; earth, air, fire, water, space. This mudra helps to bring a sense of balance and harmony. So, if I'm feeling a little out of balance, the Dharma Pravartana mudra is a great focus.

Figure 4. Dharma Pravartana Mudra.

Svasti mudra is a gesture of taking your power back and putting up a shield of protection to protect you from negative energy. If you feel that you've come under psychic attack or feel out of sorts, then this mudra will really help. At first, when you use it, you may feel a little tense. Allow your power to overflow and relax your shoulders. As you focus on the mudra and how powerful you are at protecting yourself from unseen energy, know that it is so.

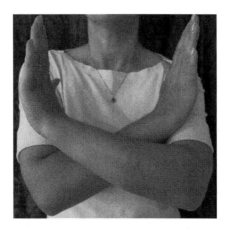

Figure 5. Svasti Mudra.

Sometimes our own limiting beliefs can creep in when we don't have our guard up. In order to combat these, the Gupta mudra gives us protection from our own limiting beliefs. This allows us the opportunity in meditation to analyse and feel why we have these limiting beliefs and help us to move forward from them.

Figure 6. Gupta Mudra.

If you are doing deep inner work and know that you need to let go of certain people, emotions, and attachments, then the Pranidhana mudra will assist you in releasing and letting go of all that no longer serves your greatest and highest good. This mudra can be deeply relaxing, so take care if your blood pressure runs low or if you are pregnant.

Figure 7. Pranidhana Mudra.

Finally, my favourite, and for me the easiest to remember, is the Ushas mudra. This beautiful mudra assists you in being open to new possibilities. How awesome is that. It's important to live in the present, but also, this mudra is an absolute gem when it comes to manifesting.

Figure 8. Ushas Mudra.

15

Journaling

Journaling is most definitely a very powerful manifestation tool. Journaling is the process of writing down your thoughts and feelings. It allows you to gain clarity and assists with the creation of your desires. You can use journaling to essentially write your new reality into existence.

I recently had an intuitive reading, and I highly recommend this experience for anyone that is considering it. One of the things that came through for me was how powerful it is for me to journal. I was told that my intentions manifest themselves much quicker when I physically write them down. It was such an incredible experience. What better way to learn about which manifesting tools work best for you than being told by your spiritual team? Having been given this knowledge, I have made it a priority to make sure that I journal absolutely every day without fail. I have incorporated it into my morning routine to ensure that this does happen. Of course, you can journal at any time of the day that best suits you and your daily routine.

All of the journaling techniques that we will discuss aid your manifestation process in their own individual ways. You may find that you resonate with certain journaling techniques more than others. As a result, you may manifest your desires faster using these techniques because you are more likely to be consistent with their use.

Gratitude Journaling

As previously mentioned in the gratitude stage of The Nine Code of Fidelity[a] and the gratitude chapter of this book, one form of journaling is gratitude journaling. Having gratitude in the present moment and feeling it every day is essential. Absolutely every morning, just before I eat my breakfast, I play the frequency of gratitude, open my gratitude journal and write down everything I am grateful for. Whether it be the things that I am grateful for that are presently in my life or the things that I am manifesting into my life as if already manifested. For example, I am always so grateful for my perfect health and for my family and friends.

When journaling, neither your subconscious mind nor the Universe actually knows the difference between the gratitude you have for your current reality and that for which you are manifesting, so write it into existence! If you truly feel gratitude for your desires, then your subconscious mind believes it.

I find that gratitude journaling is the best type of journaling when you live such a productive lifestyle, as it can be as short or as long as you like. This form of journaling doesn't take as long as others, so it is much easier to make time for, and thus is much easier to stick to a routine of journaling. You might personally find that it works better for you and your lifestyle to journal first thing in the morning, as soon as you wake up, whilst you eat your breakfast, or before you go to sleep. Once you find where journaling fits in well to your everyday routine, it will be much easier for you to journal consistently, and consistency is key.

Example Entry

- I am grateful for a lovely morning walk in nature.
- I am grateful for my amazing friends and family.
- I am grateful for my perfect health.
- I am grateful for the sunny weather.
- I am grateful for the number of great restaurants that are on my doorstep.
- I am grateful that I have multiple streams of income.
- I am grateful that I am abundant in all aspects of my life.

Day in the Life Journaling

Another journaling technique is to script a day in your life but from the perspective of the version of yourself that has already manifested your desires. A day in your dream life, so to speak. This type of journaling is also known as future scripting. This technique tends to take significantly longer than gratitude journaling, as you can sit and write for hours, going into every little detail of your ideal day. In terms of the level of detail and specificity that you give, do whatever resonates with you. You may feel drawn to give lots of specific details for some aspects whilst feeling drawn to give fewer details for other aspects. It is a great technique to use to visualise your desires as if they are already present in your reality. You really do end up getting lost in the moment whilst writing.

Due to the lengthiness of this form of journaling, it takes a little more preplanning to fit it into your day. I would suggest setting a time limit and writing what you can in that amount of time. This way, you are more likely to incorporate this technique into your day, as setting twenty minutes aside may feel more achievable than an hour. Generally, I attempt to mix it up with the techniques I use by doing the day in the life technique once a week as it goes into more detail, and the gratitude journaling the rest of the time. I find that this is what works best for me and my lifestyle, but you might find that you have the time within your day to journal for longer.

When journaling your ideal day in the life, you should make sure you use all of your senses; what can you hear, taste, touch and smell, not just what can you see. If you are manifesting a new car, you might write about how it feels to be driving the car, what you can hear, and you might even stop to put fuel in the car. Really envision the car as being yours. I write my day in the life in the present tense, as if I am experiencing it in that moment. Whereas Alexa writes it in the past tense as if she is sitting in bed at the end of the day writing about what happened during her day. Both of these methods work equally well. Use your intuition to determine which you prefer to do. The key is that you really envision yourself living that life, and your mind will believe that you are. You have to truly believe that this is your life and that you already possess everything that you are writing about. It is important that you use either past or present tense, but not future tense. If you write about having a specific something in the future, the day might never present itself as it will always be in the future.

Example Entry Excerpt

This morning I woke up in my huge bed in my bedroom of my amazing home. I could hear the birds singing outside the window and see the light coming through the curtains as I woke. I am so grateful that this is how I am awoken. I woke up around 05:30 am and then meditated before heading downstairs to the kitchen for breakfast. I opened the curtains in the kitchen and then the back door to let in some fresh air. It was a very crisp and autumnal feeling morning. I made myself porridge with cacao, banana, peanut butter and crushed hazelnuts. I also made a cup of tea, and took my breakfast to the living room to eat it. After breakfast, I went upstairs to get dressed for the day. Once dressed, I headed for a walk around the local park, and then I met Sally for lunch at a local restaurant...

Reframe Your Day Journaling

Another journaling technique is to rewrite your day the way that you feel it should have happened. Of course, you should always acknowledge the lesson you have learnt from your day not going as planned. After all, everything happens for a reason. Once acknowledgements have been made, if your day didn't go as planned or someone had a negative reaction to something, you can rewrite the day how it should have gone. Instead of dwelling on the day that you have had, you can rewrite it step by step to ensure you have a much more positive outlook on the day. The more you dwell on something, the more of that specific thing you will attract into your life. By rewriting your day in a positive way, you will be sure to attract more positivity into your life. By changing your outlook, you can and will change your life.

Example Entry

I woke up later than normal this morning which meant that I couldn't work out before going to work. My body must have needed the rest, and I am glad that I listened to it. By resting this morning, I felt much more energised and was able to work out after I had finished at the office. When I got to work this morning, my manager gave me an enormous workload with a very short deadline. However, he clearly thought that I was capable of achieving the task at hand. I actually finished the task with time to spare—what an accomplishment!

Trigger and Forgiveness Journaling

This type of journaling is brilliant for gaining clarity surrounding self-limiting beliefs in order to release them. When you are triggered by something, acknowledge the situation that triggered you. This could be something someone has said, or fears that come to mind when you think about your desires. By doing this, you allow yourself to begin the process of healing rather than ignoring the situation and suppressing the associated emotion.

Begin journaling by writing down the situation that triggered you and the thoughts you had as a result of the situation. From this you can determine the underlying self-limiting belief. This may be one or multiple self-limiting beliefs, so write down what comes to mind. Once you have identified the self-limiting belief, you should determine how it is both serving you and how it is affecting you moving forward. You can then consider the accuracy of the belief. Is it true? Are there examples that you can think of that refute this belief? What is the actual truth? Following this you should forgive yourself for holding onto this belief and release it from yourself. This can be done by using the Ho'oponopono forgiveness prayer; I am sorry, please forgive me, I love you, thank you. This then allows you to reframe the belief and use tools such as affirmations to reprogramme your subconscious mind.

Example Entry

Trigger: Someone saying that they intend to gain five new customers a week.

Thought: How are they capable of doing that? What makes them think they can do that?

Self-limiting belief: I'm not capable or worthy of creating my desires.

How does it serve me: I get to stay safe in my comfort zone.

How does it affect me moving forward: I don't get to live my dream life.

Accuracy: Many people have created their desires. If they are capable of it then so am I.

Forgive: I am sorry. Please forgive me. I love you. Thank you.

Reframe: I am fully capable and worthy of creating all of my desires.

16

MOON PHASES & CEREMONIES

What Are the Moon Phases?

There are eight moon phases:

1. New Moon
2. Waxing Crescent
3. First Quarter
4. Waxing Gibbous
5. Full Moon
6. Waning Gibbous
7. Third Quarter
8. Waning Crescent

Throughout the times, farmers have planted seeds based on the moon phase to gain significantly increased yield. It is also well documented that the Royals and governments use astronomy and moon phases when making important decisions. The Astronomer Royal is an award given to an eminent astronomer who is expected to advise the Monarch on all matters astronomical. Whether it is an important meeting or a lifechanging decision, these will all be scheduled depending on the astronomy and moon phases. In addition, it is very well documented that millionaires don't use astrology billionaires do.

There is some very powerful magic that can be harnessed for the good of all when utilising astronomy. I would advise that if you want to look more closely at astronomy, then there are some amazing professional astronomers that I recommend you consult. For the purpose of creating and manifesting, I will discuss the key moon phases and rituals.

Full Moon Manifestation

The full moon should be used for removing and releasing all that no longer serves you. Whether it's a person or situation, an emotion or something else that you no longer resonate with and want out of your life.

You will need:

- A candle (I prefer to use a white candle as this signifies new beginnings and purity for me)
- Incense (I prefer to use frankincense or dragon's blood)
- A besom, broom or brush.
- Paper and a pen

Find a relaxing place outside in the garden or yard. Use the besom to cleanse the area physically and spiritually of low energies. As you sweep, have an intention that you are removing low energies from the space—clearing and cleansing. Sit down comfortably, and light your candle and incense stick. Write down everything that you are releasing and cleansing.

Say a few words out loud or in your mind.

"I now choose to release all feelings, all emotions, and all situations that no longer serve my greatest and highest good.

I give them over to the Universe for
transformation into positive energies.
I am free.
I am empowered.
I am worthy of the most incredible life.
I give thanks to the Universe for all that I am."

Then burn the paper carefully and sweep away the embers with the besom or broom. You may also prefer to blow the embers out into the ether. If you know which element your astrological sign resonates with (earth, air, water or fire), you may wish to use this element within your ritual. So, after burning the paper, you may wish to bury the embers (earth element) or place them in a stream (water element) or, as I do, use air to blow it on its way (air element). With the knowledge that the Universe and the moon have transmuted all those energies and situations that no longer serve you, you can move forward along your spiritual journey.

New Moon Manifestation

The new moon is perfect for starting new projects, signing contracts, or moving house. It's also a great time to harness the energy that has been created throughout the moon phase and amplify your creation or your manifestation.

You will need:

- A candle. You may wish to pick a candle colour that resonates with what you are creating.

Pink or red: Love
Green: Money or abundance
Yellow: Knowledge
Orange: Happiness and joy
Black: Protection
Purple: Esoteric knowledge and wisdom
Blue: Truth
Gold, silver and white are very high frequency colours and should be used intuitively.

- Incense
- Besom or broom
- Paper and a pen

Again, find yourself a comfortable space in the garden or yard where you won't be disturbed. Cleanse the space with the besom, and light the candle and incense. Write your intentions for what it is that you are creating. Read the list out loud to the Universe and moon. I want you to really visualise and feel as if it has already occurred. Feel the happiness, the joy, and the excitement that you will feel when it has happened. Burn the list and use whatever element your birthdate resonates with. For me, I then use air by sweeping the embers or blowing them away. Give thanks to the Universe for your incredible life with much love and gratitude.

Cacao Ceremony

A cacao ceremony is an ancient ceremony that originated from tribes in Central and South America. During the ceremony, you consume a drink known as ceremonial cacao, which amongst other things, helps to enhance your creativity and connection to your higher self and release self-limiting beliefs.

I use ceremonial cacao as a tool for manifestation and releasing all that no longer serves my highest good, often in conjunction with the moon phases. During a new moon, I will conduct a cacao ceremony to set my intentions for my goals and desires. Whereas, during a full moon, I will conduct a cacao ceremony to release all that no longer serves me.

In order to conduct a cacao ceremony, you will need organic ceremonial grade cacao and plant-based milk or water. Firstly, chop or grate 15-30g of ceremonial grade cacao, depending on your preference. Then heat enough milk for your receptacle in a saucepan until it is hot but not boiling. Gently add the chopped or grated ceremonial cacao and stir with a wooden spoon. It is important that if you are setting your intention for your goals and desires, you stir clockwise. Whereas, if you are setting your intention for releasing all that no longer serves you, you should stir anticlockwise. After all of the ceremonial grade cacao has dissolved, pour it into your receptacle. Take a teaspoon and focus on your intention for the cacao ceremony whilst stirring your drink in the appropriate direction. Sit in a quiet place where you can contemplate your intention whilst you consume the drink.

Sigils

Sigils are symbols that allow you to focus your power and intention in order to create your desires. There are many sigils created by others that are readily available for you to activate and use, or you can create your own. The sigil is a representation of a specific desire and holds the energy of your intention for that desire. For each different desire, you would use a different sigil. Sigils work by tapping into your subconscious mind, rather than your conscious, analytical mind. Below, you will find three sigils. From top to bottom, the intention for each sigil is:

- My business is more and more successful each day
- Prosperity
- I am successful

Figure 9. Examples of sigils.

How to Create a Sigil

There are many different ways that you can create, charge and activate a sigil. As such, I will outline below how I create, charge and activate my sigils.

1. Write down what it is that you desire to bring into your reality. This could be in the form of a statement such as "I am financially abundant" or as a short phrase such as "spiritual protection". If you are writing a sentence, ensure that you write it in a positive manner and in the present tense. You can use the goal that you outlined in the goal setting stage of The Nine Code of Fidelity[a] to help you form your statement or phrase.

2. Cross out all of the vowels and all of the repeating letters within your sentence or short phrase.

3. Use the remaining letters to create your sigil. You can arrange the letters in any way that resonates with you. This may be:

- Enlarged or minimized
- The correct way up, upside down or sideways
- Overlapping other letters
- Capital or lowercase

Take your time and have fun with the process. If you arrange the letters in a certain way, and you don't like it or resonate with it, then feel free to start again and rearrange them. I often rearrange the letters a few times before I am happy with the outcome.

4. Once you are happy with the sigil you have created, I would suggest redrawing it onto your chosen material, such as paper, wood or a candle. The material that you use will depend on the activation method you choose, which we will discuss below. This also applies to any sigils made by others that you are using. As you draw your sigil, focus on your intention behind it in order to charge it.

5. In addition to charging your sigil whilst redrawing it, I also like to simply gaze upon it whilst focusing on my intention for the sigil. You can also meditate on the sigil and visualise the desired outcome of using it. These are all great ways to charge your sigil with your intention.

How to Activate a Sigil

After you have redrawn and charged your sigil, it is time to activate it. This can be done by either active activation or passive activation. The general process of activation essentially releases the energy out into the universe that you have charged the sigil with.

Active activation releases all of the energy of your intention that the sigil holds in one quick process. You then let it go and forget about it. This is done by destroying the sigil, which is most commonly through the act of burning it. Take your charged sigil that has been drawn on a piece of paper and safely burn it, releasing the energy and intention that it holds out into the universe. Take the ashes from the sigil and bury them in the soil, let them blow away in the wind, or dispose of them in any other way that resonates with you. There are many other methods of active activation, including drawing the sigil in the sand and blowing it away, and drawing it on a piece of paper and dissolving it in water. This type of activation is great for sigils where your intention is specific to something that is short-term, and doesn't require your energy daily to accomplish the goal. This could be a sigil for confidence at an interview, clarity of speech, or to make a good decision.

Passive activation releases the energy of your intention that the sigil holds slowly overtime as the sigil is not destroyed. There are many methods of passive activation that you can use, which involve placing the sigil in an area where you will see it often. You may draw the sigil on a piece of paper or wood and stick it on the wall, carve it into a candle, write it on your skin, make artwork for your home that incorporates it, or have it as your phone or computer background. This type of activation is great for sigils that are needed for a longer length of time. This could be sigils such as those for abundance, protection and success. As the energy held within the sigil releases over time, you may need to occasionally recharge the sigil with the same intention.

17

HYPNOSIS

Hypnosis is an immensely powerful tool on many levels, particularly for reprogramming the subconscious belief system, and rewiring that information in a positive manner. It can also be used for regressing to the root cause of a problem, emotion or belief in order to undertake the necessary healing work and forgiveness that may be required to move forward in life. Some hypnotherapists also work in a 'content free' way. This means that the root cause doesn't necessarily need to be known.

Hypnosis in Utero

It is understood by science that during the last trimester of a mother's pregnancy, the fetus is undergoing a tremendous amount of growth and development of neural pathways. During this stage of development, the fetus is primarily in the delta brainwave. The delta brain wave frequency is the deepest level of sleep, and allows for very deep levels of calmness. It is associated with the empathy and intuitive side of the brain. This brainwave allows the baby to connect on a very deep level to everything in the external environment. The baby also connects to its mother deeply and feels everything she is feeling. This has become very evident from hypnosis sessions.

It would be idyllic to think that all pregnant mothers are financially stable, have great relationships and that it is a planned pregnancy where she feels empowered to make informed decisions about her care and that of her unborn baby. However, my past experience as a midwife and with three children of my own tells me that sometimes, new mothers feel confused about their care. They can feel overwhelmed by the tests and procedures now routinely offered in allopathic medicine; let alone a lack of control and power around their own body. There is often fear around medical procedures such as ultrasound scans that are specifically looking for anomalies or deformities, and blood tests looking for markers and abnormal results—to name but a few.

They may be fearful that they don't have the financial stability to bring a baby into this world. They may be having relationship problems and not trust men, or perhaps the pregnancy was a surprise, and a termination was considered. The baby, in utero, will be very aware of all this on a subconscious level. The mother's emotional experience of childbirth may also be transferred to the baby and have an effect later in life. From my personal experience, I found that I was still connected to my mother's fear of induction of labour. This emotion was being held in my solar plexus as if it was my own. With guidance during hypnosis, I was able to remove this fear.

I have found that clients will also regress into utero during hypnosis and have a realisation that many emotions or self-limiting beliefs they have been carrying are not theirs. They are, in fact, their mother's feelings or even other ancestors' feelings. To forgive and release that emotion, they must undertake healing on an ancestral level, and the etheric cord must be cut. This allows the soul to understand that it is not their emotion to hold.

Childhood Conditioning

As the baby grows and develops, the brain wave patterns alter to that of theta and alpha. A child, from birth up until around six-to-seven years old, spends the majority of its time in the theta brain wave, or a waking hypnotic state. This means that whatever the child is exposed to within their environment, is downloaded to shape the programming of their subconscious mind. This could be anything that they feel, see, hear or smell. This subconscious programming may be responsible for future phobias, self-limiting beliefs, and how they see the world and navigate their life. Some examples of subconscious programming resulting in self-limiting beliefs that I often see include:

- Your parents always telling other people that you are shy
- A teacher telling you what you will or will not become
- Someone telling you that you always behave a certain way
- Someone commenting on the way you physically look

It's important that you know that whatever someone thinks about you is a reflection of their own self-limiting beliefs and how they view themselves. They are projecting their own self-limiting beliefs upon you. However, as an impressionable child, your subconscious mind is like a sponge. You absorb everything you are exposed to, whether you realise it or not. As an adult, you should choose your words wisely, even if said in jest or from a caring place. What you project out into the world is a reflection of your inner world. You are a powerful multidimensional being, and you are capable of being and doing anything that you believe is possible.

Past Life Regression

The root cause of any issue may either be in this lifetime or another lifetime. Contrary to popular belief, time is not linear. What many refer to as past lives are simply other lifetimes that you are living simultaneously. Generally, most people will only consciously remember the life that this part of their soul is living now. However, on a soul level, you may become aware of phobias and emotions that appear to have no root cause in your current lifetime. Therefore, there is still healing or forgiveness to be completed from a different lifetime. This can affect the life that you are currently experiencing by creating self-limiting beliefs until it is understood and healed. For the simplicity of understanding throughout, we will refer to other lifetimes as past lives.

It may be that in a past life, a vow or a covenant was made, and the soul in your current incarnation is abiding by that promise. For instance, it may be a vow of poverty that was taken in a previous lifetime. This then results in a self-limiting belief surrounding abundance in your current lifetime if it is not revoked.

Identify, Process & Reprogramme Self-limiting Beliefs

So how can you use hypnosis to identify, process and reprogramme your subconscious mind of all those self-limiting beliefs?

There are various hypnosis techniques that can be used to achieve this, including regression and content free hypnosis. Hypnosis isn't a magic wand, and you must be willing to alter your mindset, thoughts and feelings. Whilst hypnosis can be used to assist in the reframing of self-limiting beliefs, ultimately the power is within you to create change.

Identify and Process

Firstly, you need to identify the self-limiting belief you wish to reframe. Sit and meditate on the particular area that you would like to change. Perhaps it is your beliefs surrounding money that you wish to change. Which memories come to mind when you think about money whilst meditating? Were you told that "Money doesn't grow on trees"? Or perhaps "We can't afford that. Stop being greedy". All of these are self-limiting beliefs. Once you have identified the self-limiting belief, you can then use the Ho'oponopono forgiveness prayer. It is outlined in stage five of The Nine Code of Fidelity[a]. This allows you to forgive yourself, your ancestors and your past lives for self-limiting beliefs.

Sometimes you don't know why you appear to have self-limiting beliefs surrounding certain areas. You may have been triggered by something that brought a particular emotion to the surface. When you contemplate this, you may feel uncertain as to why there is an underlying self-limiting belief. For instance, you may have been triggered by something that brought the feeling of worthlessness to the surface. However, on contemplation, you feel there are no logical reasons as to why you would feel this way. This is where the help of a regression hypnotherapist comes in. In particular, current life and past life regression can be used as a tool to assist the client in locating and removing any self-limiting beliefs. Often, a client will intuitively know that they have a self-limiting belief around a certain area but do not have any idea why.

During hypnosis, it is possible to go to the origin of the feeling that anchored the self-limiting belief in your subconscious mind. This can be found regardless of the lifetime it originated from.

There may be forgiveness and healing work to be done in that lifetime to process the emotion. This then allows you to see the self-limiting belief from a new perspective and subsequently reframe it.

A few sessions immediately spring to mind. One is a session where a client was unable to retain or save money. In hypnosis, I asked him to go to the origin of the feeling associated with this. He found himself in the body of an orphaned Victorian boy, who was barefoot with rags for clothes and starving. The client felt that they did not want to be like the wealthy people who mistreated others. As a result, he had put limitations upon how much money he felt he could have in this lifetime in order to view himself as a good person. Of course, the client could now see that having wealth does not make you a bad person, and that this belief was not benefiting their current lifetime. You can indeed use wealth to benefit many other people. By viewing this lifetime from a new perspective, the client was able to heal, forgive and locate the feeling in their current body to release it.

There was another session with a client that had severe recurring back discomfort with no known physical cause. During a hypnosis session, I asked her to focus on the back discomfort and feel the associated emotion. I then asked the client to go to the origin of this feeling. She found herself in a very hot country doing heavy manual labour in the body of an elderly man. The man felt frustration, anger and resentment towards his employer as he felt he had to do very hard work to earn very little. During the session, the client was able to see what she had learnt from that lifetime, giving her a new perspective. She could see that there was no benefit to holding the belief that she must work hard to make money in her current lifetime. She was then able to forgive herself for holding onto the emotions that were affecting her current lifetime and remove them, allowing herself to heal. By allowing this healing to take place and releasing the low frequency emotions, the client's frequency naturally raised.

The final session that springs to mind was with a client that was almost crippled with neurological pain and discomfort. It is my firm belief that your body never wants to hurt you. Your soul uses discomfort in your body to communicate to you that something is amiss. During this session, I asked permission to speak to the client's higher self and determined that the cause of the pain was grief from her grandfather's death years ago. I asked if there was anything that she needed to tell her grandfather, which gave her closure. During the session, her grandfather was able to remove and transmute the grief that had been stored within her bioenergetic field. After the session, all physical manifestations of discomfort had resolved themselves. As a result of removing the low frequency emotion of grief, the client's frequency raised naturally.

These are just a few of many examples of emotions that can anchor a self-limiting belief into the subconscious mind.

Reprogramme

In order to reprogramme the subconscious mind, you can use positive subliminal messages that you listen to whilst you sleep. You naturally fall into the theta brain wave state or hypnosis at least twice a day—just as you're nodding off to sleep and that brief period of time when you're waking from a deep sleep. It's these theta brain waves that you want to take advantage of.

Take, for example, the self-limiting belief that you have to work hard to make money. Reframe this belief to form the following affirmations:

- Money flows to me with ease
- I find joy and happiness in all of the work that I do
- I am abundant in all areas of my life

- Each day I am able to help more and more people with my never-ending stream of abundance
- Money flows to me like crazy

Make the affirmations believable for you. Start small if you need to, but make it believable. Use your phone or recording device to record yourself speaking three to six positive affirmations that refute your self-limiting beliefs. Then create an audio file that has these affirmations repeated for an hour. Be certain to frame the words of your affirmations positively and in the present tense. Then listen to the recording just as you're nodding off to sleep and again on waking. Keep using the recording until you feel your mindset has changed.

18

Spiritual Protection

What is Spiritual Protection?

Spiritual protection is the practice of holding the belief that you are mentally, physically and emotionally protected from low frequency and dark force energies that have been created by the collective consciousness. This may be as simple as knowing that your heart energy protects you, or it may be a more complex ritual using specific tools for protection.

Whether you feel you require spiritual protection or not depends on what you believe and feel and, therefore, what you manifest. Remember that you create your reality. If you believe, without a doubt, that you are completely protected from dark force energies without using any protection tools, then this is your truth. However, if there is any doubt in your belief of complete self-protection, then I would recommend using tools for spiritual protection. By intentionally using these tools, you are focusing and channelling your creative power and energy and directing it in order to manifest spiritual protection around you. Tune into your inner knowing during meditation, and ask your spiritual team if you should use any type of protection when working within the spiritual realm.

Many spiritual healers and workers, including myself, find these tools to be particularly beneficial to their daily routines. If you choose not to use spiritual protection tools, ensure that this decision comes from a place of truth and not from your ego. From my experience with clients, I have had to assist in removing dark force attachments that were causing emotional and physical problems. In many cases, it was a result of not having spiritual protection in place due to an ego-based decision and becoming a vibrational match to that energy momentarily. It is essential to emphasise the importance of ensuring that your frequency is high when undertaking spiritual work. You attract that which you are a vibrational match to. When you are feeling low frequency, you become a vibrational match to lower frequency energies. It is, therefore, better to avoid doing spiritual work until you have raised your frequency.

As many of you are aware, you chose to incarnate at this time of ascension in order to raise the frequency of the collective consciousness and the planet to the energies of the fifth dimension. As per the universal Law of Polarity, where there is light, there is dark. Within the collective consciousness, there are dark, low frequency energies that may attempt to take you off of your spiritual path to ascension. This is why it is essential to take control of your frequency and use spiritual protection tools when needed.

Layers of the Aura

Your aura is the energetic field around your body that holds information about your emotions and physical and mental health. It is also known as the bioenergetic field or biofield. Your aura changes from moment to moment, depending on your thoughts and feelings.

146

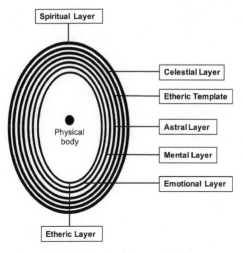

Figure 10. A representation of the layers of the aura.

There are seven energy layers around your body that make up your aura. From the closest to your body, moving outwards, they are:

1. **Etheric layer**: This is the first layer of energy that resides closest to your physical body. It is approximately 4 cm above your skin.
2. **Emotional layer:** This layer resides next to the etheric layer and houses your emotions and feelings.
3. **Mental layer:** This is the next layer after the emotional layer. It houses the energy of your thoughts and how you process information.
4. **Astral layer:** Following the mental layer is the astral layer. It is the layer that bridges the physical realm with the spiritual realm.
5. **Etheric template:** This layer is the fifth layer of your aura and is seen as the blueprint of the physical body.
6. **Celestial layer:** This layer resides next to the etheric template layer and houses your spiritual connection.

7. **Spiritual layer:** This is the final layer of your aura, and it protects all other layers of your aura.

Your aura is essentially your natural energetic defence system when it is healthy and strong. If your frequency becomes lower, this can cause the layers of your aura to weaken or tear. As a result, other energies may be able to gain access to the layers of your aura and become attached.

Attachments

There are many forms of spiritual attachment that can cause various mental and physical symptoms to occur. Sometimes it is an attachment such as a dark energy or astral parasite feeding off the client's light. These energies often hiss, spit and shout profanities at me as they have been discovered in the client's bioenergetic field during hypnosis. Some attachments may make the client feel their anger, despair and resentment, ultimately keeping them in that low vibrational place. These feelings can often affect a client mentally and physically. Another form of attachment is an earthbound spirit that is someone who has died but not crossed over. This may be due to confusion and fear at the point of leaving the body after death, resulting in attachment to a person vibrating at a similar frequency. Occasionally there may be an implant or nanobot identified in the bioenergetic field that has been placed there by galactic beings. This type of attachment is very rarely negative in nature, but rather used to transfer information to and from your galactic family. Finally, etheric cords and hooks may be discovered during a client's body scan in hypnosis. These cords or hooks may lead to a person, memory or situation that is somehow draining the client of energy. The client is able to take back their power and cut the cord or remove the hook.

As we are all part of the collective consciousness, even clients who don't believe in attachments may find that, in hypnosis, they are able to sense the energy of an attachment. At some point their frequency had become a vibrational match to that of the attachment attracting it into their bioenergetic field.

There are various things that can potentially expose you to an energy attachment by either lowering your frequency or altering your cognitive state. These include trauma, alcohol, drugs, general anaesthetic, organ transplant, blood transfusion, passing out, black magic, depression and low frequency emotions. These may result in a tear in your auric field, which then allows etheric entities to attach.

Of course, we create everything that we experience within our reality. If someone has an attachment of any description, they have created that or allowed that into their bioenergetic field to learn something. This allows their soul to evolve even more. As humans, we package things neatly into good or bad experiences, but in reality, they are all experiences that we have chosen to have. During a hypnosis session, it is imperative that we remove these attachments that may be affecting us. Before they are relocated, it is important that we find out why and how they attached and if they have been affecting the client emotionally or physically. This allows the client to take their power back to remove and relocate the energy attachment that does not belong there.

It's important to remember that everyone is from the light, and my incredible teachers have always taught me that everyone will return to the light. Ultimately, we all want freedom, and we don't want to be controlled. Using skilful techniques, it is possible to converse with these attachments regardless of their origin, and to relocate them to the place where they belong within the light. It can be very empowering for the client to see the energy that is attached. They can also gain an understanding as to why, when and where it attached, and with guidance, assist this energy to its place within the light.

Curses, Hexes and Psychic Attack

Some traditions and cultures believe very strongly in the power of curses, hexes and psychic attack. Many years ago, a client asked me if I believed in curses. My response was that it did not matter what I believed, as it was what she believed that ultimately creates her reality. If she believes in curses, then that is her truth.

It is important to know that the curse, hex or psychic attack only exists in your reality because you have given your power away to it, and you believe that the person instigating it is more powerful than you. You believe that it can have an effect on you, and so it does. After a series of events, I woke up one morning to an abundance of beetles in my kitchen that I had never seen before. Now, given previous events, I could have very easily slipped into fear and panic that this was a form of psychic attack and focused my energy on it. I chose not give my power or energy away to it. I put all the beetles out in garden, and that was the end of that. I made this decision from a place of knowing that I am the most powerful creator of my reality, so any dark energy that was sent my way was simply returned.

When the power of curses, hexes and psychic attack is taught to you from a young age, it may be more difficult to believe that you can indeed take your power back. You are the powerful creator of your reality and life experience. Stop putting people on pedestals and believing that they are more powerful than you in creating your own life. If this triggers you, then you should consider who you are freely giving your power away to. If you do believe that you have been cursed or hexed, I would suggest seeking help to have it removed through a spiritual hypnotherapist or person that practices such removal. When you believe curses, hexes or psychic attack to be your truth, you have allowed it to manifest in your reality and, in effect, nominalised it. This is why it is important to firstly remove it and then learn how to take your power back and not allow others to make you feel any less than the divine, powerful being that you are.

How to Protect Your Energy

Through many years of experience working in the spiritual field, I have chosen to use many tools of protection to protect my energy. I have created a routine with these tools to provide optimum protection for my clients and me. It is imperative with the type of work that I do that I hold a high frequency, protected space for my clients at all times. By using these tools, I unequivocally believe that I am protected, and that any clients that I see are also protected. Through dedicated spiritual practices, you are able to develop your innate ability to feel and sense energies, and in particular those that are attempting to access your energy. You can also sense if you are allowing your energy to be drained by someone else.

Each morning on waking and right before I start meditation, I connect to the centre of the earth and bring the beautiful energy up. In doing so, I create a pillar of silver white protective energy around myself that goes all the way up to what I perceive as Divine Source energy. This pillar of protective light surrounds me and protects me from unseen energies. Before seeing a client in clinic, I will boost this energy and project it out into the room, forming a layer of protection over the healing room. I will also bless and dedicate the room to healing in the highest frequency of love. I have a small dish of salt in each of the four corners of the healing room and the house to provide protection from any unwanted energies. Often clients enter the space that may have been through trauma or life lessons of a low frequency that need to be healed. To provide extra protection and raise the frequency whilst assisting with this, I have crystals in the healing room such as rose quartz, clear quartz, shungite and selenite. I also wear specific crystals that help to protect my bioenergetic field, such as labradorite, ruby and obsidian. In addition, there are many sigils and ancient symbols, such as the triquetra, that can be used for protection. These allow you to focus and harness your innate power. One of the sigils that I use within the healing room harnesses my intention that all negative energy is banished.

The easiest way to ensure that you are not a vibrational match to lower frequency energies is to ensure that your frequency is high. Do things daily that make you feel high frequency emotions such as love, joy and gratitude. Take time to keep grounded to Mother Earth and connected to Divine Source. You should also set strong, healthy boundaries. Your energy is precious so ensure that you say no to anything that doesn't resonate with you. If there is an event that you feel obligated to attend, but don't resonate with, such as a family event, envision a shield or mirror around yourself to deflect any energies that are not of love. It is important that you don't lower your frequency to make another person feel better. Instead, be supportive whilst keeping your frequency high, and teach them to raise their frequency using the tools of creation.

Another tool that I recommend using for spiritual protection is to envision yourself inside a pyramid or bubble of white light and set the intention that you are protected from all that does not serve your highest good. This is a really simple but effective tool. I personally do this before I do any spiritual practice, such as meditation or connecting to the energy of others, as well as when I feel it necessary during the day and before I sleep at night. This reminds me of a time when I visited the hellfire caves, which are known to be the historic meeting place of a secret society that conducted satanic rituals. Of course, the caves are now open to the public. As we approached the inner temple, there was a change in energy that felt heavy and low frequency. Instead of going to a low frequency place of fear, I simply placed a bubble of protection around us. As soon as I did this, the music in the cave turned off, and it went completely silent. It felt as if this was symbolic of the fact that I had placed the protection around us. This reaffirmed to me that this tool of protection really does help to focus my power to provide protection.

It's very important to protect your bioenergetic field both during the daytime and nighttime. Many may be accustomed to protecting themselves during the daytime but may not be protecting themselves at nighttime. Many of you reading this book are starseeds which means that you are most likely doing work on other planets or dimensions during your sleep. Either way, I would recommend placing protection around yourself before going to sleep. I recall one evening many years ago where I went to bed with a lower frequency than usual. This was a result of being triggered by something during the day that I hadn't properly processed. During the night, I suddenly became aware of a very dark mass of energy to my left-hand side. I felt myself being dragged diagonally out of my body towards the dark mass. I was almost completely out of my body when I saw a flash of bright white light that brought me back into my body. The following day, I had an Akashic Record reading, and it was evident that someone had tried to take my light and remove me from my body. I was told that when I was a teenager, my spiritual team had worked on my physical and etheric body to prevent anyone from removing my light, as they had seen the timeline where this was attempted. The lesson that I learnt from this situation was the importance of protecting my physical and etheric body whilst sleeping. This can be done using the same tools that you would use to protect yourself during the daytime. It is also useful to set the intention that you do not consent to anyone accessing your bioenergetic field at any time of the day or night.

Detecting Low Frequency Energy

Lemons are an excellent early warning device for low frequency energies present in your environment. The belief that lemons can ward off dark evil spirits goes back to time immemorial. In many Indian cultures, you can find lemons hung in the doorway of businesses to ward off evil. Certain cultures will also cut a lemon into pieces and throw it out of the door for protection. Remember that you are creating with your intent, so if you hold the belief that the lemon will ward off evil, then ward off evil it most certainly will.

Through my own experience and belief, I have found lemons to be an excellent indicator of the type of energy present in my home. I have an unwaxed lemon in a lemon dish in each room of the house, particularly in corners of the room where the energy may stagnate. There are occasions when the energy in particular areas of the home becomes low frequency. It may be that someone has been ill within the home, or perhaps there is a cluttered bedroom creating stagnant energy, a guest that has visited with low frequency energy, or even a low frequency entity that has entered the home. In a room with good, high frequency energy, the lemon will simply turn a dark yellow or brown colour and go hard like a golf ball. Once this has happened, replace it with a fresh one. If, however, there is low frequency energy present, then the lemon will rot and go green and mouldy. These low frequency energies within the home all have an impact on the bioenergetic fields of those who live there. By using lemons as an indicator of the frequency of the energy present, it enables you to take your power back and remove the low frequency energies using cleansing techniques. Once you have cleansed the area, replace the mouldy lemon with a fresh one.

Thankfully I haven't had many situations where a lemon has rotted. However, there is one particular occasion that does come to mind.

I facilitated a hypnotherapy session for a lady many years ago who was viewing a past life. During the session, a very dark energy began to speak through her. This energy was demonic in nature and verbally aggressive towards me for assisting her in removing this energy. Following the session, I quickly smudged the healing room to cleanse the energy. The following morning, I walked by the healing room door, and my guides shouted, "Lemon!". I asked what they meant, and they repeated the word again. I entered the healing room and checked the lemon on the bookcase. On initial inspection, the lemon looked perfectly fine. To my absolute horror, as I picked up the lemon, I saw that the underside was completely rotted and mouldy. This was an indication that there was low frequency energy present. My guides pointed out that the energy present in the room the day before was very low frequency, and the room had not been cleansed properly. This highlights the importance of properly cleansing your space.

How to Cleanse Your Bioenergetic Field and Environment

It is important to cleanse your bioenergetic field after being around others or after working with others and connecting energies. When your clients, friends, or family speak with you about their problems and their difficulties, you are connecting to that energy. Your body and soul will not know if it is indeed you going through this situation or whether you are merely an observer. Your body will start to react from a physiological level as if you are going through that same situation. It is, therefore, important that you remove this energy from your bioenergetic field by cleansing your energy at the end of the day. You should also remind your body that you are loved and safe, and that the situation is not yours to take on. It is essential that you do release any energy that is not your own on a regular basis in order to prevent a build-up of other people's energy within your field. There are many tools that you can use in order to cleanse your bioenergetic field and environment. Use whichever tool works best for you and your daily routine.

Smudging

One tool that you can use to cleanse your bioenergetic field and environment is smudging. Smudging is the ritualistic act whereby you burn specific sacred herbs and put your intent out into the cosmos that you are removing all that is not of the light. Smudging goes back to the indigenous tribes, where they would smudge prior to any ritual. Many of these beautiful tribes would use white sage to smudge before connecting to their ancestors or to the spirits. Smudging correctly cleanses and clears the area of low frequency energies, replenishing them with higher frequency, pure energies. From a scientific perspective, it is known that smudging with sage actually removes the positive ions that our physical bodies don't resonate with and replenishes them with negative ions, which improves the quality of the air.

There are many dried sacred herbs, kinds of wood and resins that you can use to smudge yourself and your environment:

- White Sage
- Purple Sage
- Lavender
- Eucalyptus

- Palo Santo
- Frankincense & Myrrh

How to Smudge Using Sage

You will need:

- Organic white or purple dried sage
- A 1 to 2-inch thick wooden bowl (for loose sage) or an abalone shell (for a tied bunch of sage)
- Long matches or a lighter
- A naturally fallen feather (optional)

1. Take a handful of ethically sourced, organic sage or your tied bunch of sage, and place it in your chosen receptacle. Ensure that your receptacle isn't going to burn your hand when it warms up. Many choose to use an abalone, and I've found that these are perfect if you are using a tied bunch of sage to catch any ash. However, if you are using loose dried sage, the abalone may become far too hot for you to hold. In this case, I would suggest using a 1 to 2-inch thick wooden bowl.
2. Ensure all doors and windows are closed within the room.
3. Light the sage using the long matches or lighter and gently blow on the embers until it smokes. It is important to note that if the frequency in the room is good, then the sage can be quite difficult to light. Whereas, if the energy is low frequency, the sage is much easier to light.
4. Use either your hand or a feather to gently waft the smoke as you move around the room. Ensure that the smoke permeates all corners of the room.
5. As you walk around the room wafting the smoke, use an incantation such as:

"As I smudge here this day, I command all that is not of the light to go away. Transmuting all low frequency energy over all space, time, dimension and reality. So Mote It Be."

You may prefer to call this a prayer or a mantra, but I prefer incantation because it has that magical feel to it. Remember, it is all intention. I am setting my intent that anything that is not of the light will be removed from this space and transmuted into positive energy. Now whether it is transmuted within the room or they exit out of the window when I've finished is not my concern.

6. Follow this process until the room is thick with smoke, and then place the receptacle containing the sage in a safe area to burn down or extinguish it.
7. Leave the room for at least an hour.
8. On returning, close the door quickly behind you, open all the windows and allow the smoke and low energy to be released for transmutation by the Universe. Leave the windows open for around 30 minutes, and then close the windows and use the room as normal.

This method can be adapted to whichever herb, wood or resin you choose to smudge with. If you are smudging the whole house, then do it room by room following the method above. I would suggest that you smudge your whole house at least twice a year. You can also smudge your own bioenergetic field by simply lighting the sage and carefully wafting the smoke around your body for at least two or three minutes. Use your intuition to feel when you need to smudge your own bioenergetic field. Personally, I find myself using other methods of cleansing for my bioenergetic field on a daily basis, such as tuning forks and salt baths.

Tuning Forks, Chimes and Crystal Bowls

These can be used to raise the frequency of your energy and your environment. I particularly like to use a tuning fork or crystal bowl tuned to a frequency of 432 Hz to cleanse the auric field. It is important that you use your intuition when using such tools. If you resonate with the sound of it, then go ahead and use it.

Incense and Aromatherapy Oils

Incense has been used for thousands of years in churches and temples to cleanse and clear the energy within the building for rituals.

Going back through the ages, we used plants and their extracts in order to heal and revitalise. Aromatherapy oils have a plethora of antiseptic, antibacterial and antifungal properties, as well as other proven healing properties. Both incense and aromatherapy oil aromas can affect your mood in a very positive way too. This works on the olfactory system. Basically, what you smell and breathe into your lungs has an effect on your brain on an emotional level. This, in turn, helps you to raise your frequency. The aromas that I use most often are frankincense, myrrh, sandalwood, dragon's blood, lavender and rose. Always ensure that the incense or aromatherapy oil is organic to avoid breathing in toxins.

Salt Baths

If you have been around low frequency energies, then another great way to cleanse your energy is to have a Himalayan, sea salt or Epson salt bath. This will help to remove any low frequency energies. You can also place an obsidian crystal in the bath water with you, which will help to absorb any low frequency energies. Having a salt bath is an easy, relaxing way to cleanse your bioenergetic field at the end of the day.

Hug a Tree

When you hug a tree, you can literally feel the strong energy of the tree. Connect to it and allow the lower frequency energies to flow from you into the tree and down into Gaia for transformation into positive energy. Give thanks to the tree for cleansing your energy. There is an exchange of energies that feels like connecting to Mother Earth herself, like having a huge blanket of love wrapped around you.

19

Discerning Positive Energies

Sacred Geometry and Symbols

What an interesting topic. What makes a piece of geometry sacred? Is it the mathematics behind it? Is it the people who we are told have used this symbol throughout history and that it has positive connotations? Or is it that we avoid other geometry because we are told it has negative or satanic connotations? The history, or more importantly 'his-story', is just that, an altered story. We see sacred geometry dating back to Tibet and Egypt. We often see what we may be told is sacred geometric symbols in churches and temples. How can we know which pieces of sacred geometry will help mankind?

In this age of awakening and ascension we have so much information coming at us from all angles, and at times it can be confusing. You must know that you are a powerful creator. You have the ability to create the most magnificent life and only use the tools you resonate with to create it. You are an angelic multidimensional human being in your own right. Step fully into your power and own it.

If you look at a piece of sacred geometry and it resonates with you, then use it to focus your power. Always trust your instincts. If a sacred geometric symbol doesn't resonate with you, and you may not know why, then acknowledge that feeling. Trust that feeling and perhaps don't work with that particular sacred geometric symbol at this time. This is most important with sacred geometry, as these symbols will go in through your third eye. You need to know that these symbols are for your greatest and highest good. Just because someone tells you that a piece of geometry is sacred, powerful and etheric doesn't necessarily make it so. We are at a critical time in ascension, and there is a lot of misinformation out there. There has been a battle of light and dark on earth for eons, and I am certain that there are pieces of sacred geometry placed here that could amplify our manifestations, and there are others that would intentionally hinder the process.

The way sacred geometry works is on a subliminal level. As you look at the symbol, the energy, the mathematical coding and the frequency of that image will penetrate the pineal gland and affect your mind, body, spirit and DNA. The image will also hold a frequency of its own, depending upon its creator's intent and, of course, your intent.

It is important for me to keep my frequency high and to activate all of my potential within moving forward to the 5D energies and beyond. I will not allow anything or anyone to tamper with my bioenergetic field using symbology or geometry. With that in mind, use your intuition when it comes to not only sacred geometry but everything you are inviting into your bioenergetic field. Ask yourself how does it feel to you? What do you know about it? Was it channelled? Who was it channelled by? Whatever you feel from your intuition, trust it. Your intuition will only ever guide you in a way that serves your highest good.

A piece of sacred geometry that I love to use is the Sri Yantra. I have used this sacred symbol for many years and have found that it works positively and in the best ways possible for me. The Sri Yantra has nine major interlocking triangles that surround a dot in the centre, or a Bindi. These beautiful geometric shapes are said to represent the human body and the cosmos. When I focus on the Sri Yantra, it gives me a sense of freedom and the ability to move through dimensions. When meditating with the Sri Yantra, the shapes move about as if transferring energy in and out. As this process happens, I focus on the feeling of love and gratitude for having received my desires. It is known that using the Sri Yantra in meditation activates the right hemisphere of the brain very quickly. It is the right hemisphere of the brain that is the creative side, and is responsible for images, dreams and symbols. I love the frequency and vibration of this sacred symbol, and I use it because it resonates with me. Personally, I also resonate with the numbers 3, 6 and 9, so I feel drawn to symbols that hold this energy. I love the triquetra because, for me, the symbol represents the power of three and feels very protective. This is, therefore, the intention I put behind it when I use it. Finally, I deeply resonate with the ankh symbol from ancient Egypt. It is the key of life and represents the knowledge of eternal life, with a link to a significant past life of mine.

We often see sacred geometry within nature, in the building blocks of life, atoms, and our DNA. Many believe that sacred geometry may help to amplify our frequency and therefore, our manifestations. Again, instead of allowing someone to tell you that a symbol is high frequency or holds certain magic, connect to it briefly and feel. Trust that your intuition will always guide you to the best decision that serves your highest good.

Crystals

Crystals are abundant on our amazing planet and many other planets too. There are stories of the downfall of Atlantis being partly to do with the manipulation and wrong doing of work with crystals. I remember a snippet of a lifetime in Atlantis at the downfall, and there are no earthly words to describe the devastation there. With that in mind, I am acutely aware of the power that crystals hold and how they can be used to harness or amplify energies.

Crystals are living entities, and when you hold them, you can physically feel them vibrating. It's like working with a close friend when you really start working with crystals. During hypnosis sessions, time and time again, people are shown the most beautiful crystalline planets. In fact in one of my past lives, I remember being on a crystalline planet where I was an enormous amethyst quartz. The energy and power emanating from me was incredible. I felt all of the stored information that was coming from earth and transferring to Divine Source through me.

When working with crystals, you should be drawn to the crystal you're working with. This is very much in the same way as with sacred geometry or sigils. Always use your own discernment and intuition when working with crystals. When you do, you will have the most blessed relationship with crystals. Remember to choose your crystals from ethical suppliers. This should be a company that cares about the crystals, the people mining the crystals and how they are removed from the earth. Crystals belong to the earth, and we must only ever take what we need.

When you first receive a crystal, it's important to cleanse it. This can be done in various ways, including:

- Placing the crystal under running water
- Using smoke from sage or incense
- Placing the crystal on selenite
- By burying it in the earth for a day/night

Intention is everything. As you cleanse your crystal using your chosen modality, project your thoughts that this crystal is cleared and cleansed. Please remember that there are some crystals that don't like water. For example, malachite is toxic in water, pyrite will rust in water, and selenite and labradorite will both eventually dissolve in water. For these crystals, it's better to either use smudging smoke or place them on selenite to cleanse them. Of course, selenite is a self-cleansing crystal and will cleanse itself and anything around it.

Once cleansed, it's important to programme your crystal. You must set your intention with the crystal and programme it to work only within the realms of love and for the greatest and highest good of yourself and others. The crystal will then need to be cleansed between clients if you are using it for that purpose and then recharged on a full moon. I like to put my crystals outside for the last hour before sunset on the day of a full moon and leave them outside overnight. I am aware that the moon may not be what we think it is but remember, it is all about intention. If I believe that the moon that I see can assist me in clearing, cleansing and recharging my crystals, then so mote it be.

So, once you've cleansed and programmed your crystal, how do you use it? You can use the crystal whilst you meditate lay down by placing it in your hand or on your third eye or heart chakra. You can also keep your crystals on your person. Either in the form of tumble stones in your pocket or brasier, or as jewellery from an ethical source. As long as the crystal is near or on you, it is emanating its beautiful frequency within your bioenergetic field. Crystals can also go in the bath, and their beautiful energy will be amplified in the water. Please take care not to put crystals in the bath that don't like water. I would also advise not to put perfumes and toxins in the bath, especially whilst the crystals are in there. Sea salt, Himalayan salt and Epsom salts are permitted, as this will clear your bioenergetic field whilst cleansing the crystals that are emanating their wonderful healing frequency.

There are thousands of crystals and some excellent books on this topic that give you further insight into crystals and their properties. Some crystals that I often work with and the properties that I use them for are:

- **Rose quartz:** Unconditional love
- **Clear quartz:** Amplifies your intentions
- **Selenite:** Cleanses
- **Black obsidian:** Removes and transmutes low frequency energies
- **Moldavite:** Brings in galactic assistance
- **Herkimer diamond:** Stimulates psychic abilities
- **Amethyst:** Provides protection
- **Black tourmaline:** Rebalances chakras and removes low frequency energies
- **Ruby:** Balances the heart chakra
- **Amber:** Powerful healer and chakra cleanser, and absorbs pain
- **Labradorite:** Provides protection and connects with Universal energies.
- **Green aventurine:** Removes low frequency emotions and thoughts
- **Turquoise:** Provides protection

Of course, this is not an exhaustive list. There are so many crystals that I have worked with over the years and continue to work with today that it would not be possible for me to list them all. If you find yourself drawn to a particular crystal, then have a look at its properties, and often, it is exactly what you need at that point in time.

Guides, Angels & Galactic Beings

When we decide to incarnate on Earth, we have a whole team of guides with us. I like to refer to them as my spiritual team. Whilst many people refer to their spiritual team as purely guardian angels, it can actually be comprised of many other beings too. Often, we find that our guides may also be ancestors, galactic family, those we have a soul contract with, animals or people we have incarnated with before. You may find that your guides change depending on the phase of life that you are in and the lessons that you are learning at that time. You may also find that the number of guides you have changes through the phases of your life. Your spiritual team are always there with you, watching and waiting for you to ask them for assistance. They can't assist you unless you specifically ask them for help. It is as simple as asking them for help and giving them permission to help and guide you. When you do ask for help, it is important that you are open to receiving the guidance and look out for signs and synchronicities that they may use to communicate with you. You may see particular numbers, hear a song on the radio, or see a stop or go sign—to name but a few. You may ask for a specific sign that signifies to you that the decision you are considering serves your highest good. Ultimately, when you do see signs and synchronicities, you will intuitively know that it is communication meant for you from your spiritual team. As you learn to tune into the energy of your spiritual team, you may receive thoughts and feelings from them. They are essentially communicating with you through telepathy. This should always be in a heart centred, non-invasive or non-pushy way.

Many clients have asked me about my thoughts on angels and whether or not they are actually galactic beings. An angel may be described as a beautiful energy or light descending from the heavens. This is the same description as many may give for their own galactic family or spiritual team. I do believe that angels are galactic beings, but in the same way that many of us are starseeds from other planets or planes of existence too.

I am very careful when working with any other energies, whether angelic or galactic, to only work with the energies that resonate with me. Again, I am not working with energies just because someone tells me that they are good or angelic. I will work with angelic or galactic energies because I intuitively sense the high frequency and love of their energy. If the angelic or galactic energy is a bit pushy or feels off, then I will trust my intuition and not work with it. It is that simple. Remember that we are in the middle of a spiritual war, and there may be galactic and fallen ages that will pretend to be of the light in order to spread false fear and information. Ensure that you use and trust your own intuition when considering which energies to work with and any information that others may bring.

In my study of demonology and angels, I discovered that many of the demons and dark force entities appear to be fallen angels that were once of the angelic realm. As such many of the dark force entities or demons still have angelic sounding names. These dark energies can be manipulative and disguise themselves as things they are not; a wolf in sheep's clothing. They can be tricksters. Be assured that an angel would never be pushy and would never force you to do anything. An angel has a gentle, patient and love-centred energy. If there's an energy around you, or if you call upon the assistance of an angel and the energy seems pushy or heavy, then use your protective bubble and step away from that energy. I urge you to simply use your intuition when working with or invoking any energy that is either angelic or galactic. If you are unsure, then leave well alone. It is better to not work with an energy than to work with an energy that is a trickster or manipulates you somehow.

20

Toxins

Toxins are not just simply found in the things that you physically digest. You are actually exposed to an array of toxins from various sources, which can affect you physically and energetically. This could be from company you keep, the food and drink you consume, or the environment you choose to live in. The negative effects of toxins often occur as a result of an accumulation from repeated exposure. This can be exacerbated by the fact that, as part of a modern lifestyle, you may be constantly exposed to one toxin or another. As a powerful creator, if you are at a level of higher consciousness where you truly believe that you are toxin free regardless of your environment, then this is your truth. We are all moving towards this higher level of consciousness and the realisation of our inner power. Having the knowledge of such toxins in the present moment allows you to reduce your exposure to them and ultimately detoxify to raise your frequency on your path to awakening your inner power of creation.

The Company You Keep

The people you choose to be around will have a major impact on your frequency and the way that you feel. Are they happy and joyous? Are they positive and encouraging? Do they get excited about your achievements? As your frequency rises, you will find it harder to be around people you no longer resonate with. You may find that you can longer be your true, authentic self around them. It is imperative that you do not lower your frequency to fit into the situation. You may find that you are on a different path in life to those you no longer resonate with, and that is completely normal. As you raise your frequency, you will simply attract other people of the same frequency as you. You become a vibrational match to those higher frequencies. There may be an interim where you feel that you no longer resonate with your old friends but haven't yet made new connections. Be patient, do whatever makes you feel happy and know that your tribe is on their way.

There may be events where you know that there will be people present that you don't resonate with, but you feel obligated to go. This may include the type of people who complain about everything and gossip about others. Know and accept that they are on a different path to you and that their behaviour is a reflection of their own inner beliefs. Remember that you may have once been in the same position as them on your journey to spiritual awakening. I would recommend that before attending the event, you project the light in your heart to the heart of the situation and send love to it. This will energetically alter the frequency of the situation over all space, time, dimension and reality. You can also wear a black crystal such as an obsidian or tourmaline to absorb and transmute the lower frequency energies. Remember that you control how you respond to a situation and, indeed, the effect you allow it to have on yourself. Choose to focus on the positive aspects of the situation and see it from this perspective.

Food

In simple terms, you are what you eat, and food will either raise or lower your frequency. Consuming high vibrational foods is essential to keeping a high frequency.

Fruits and vegetables are high frequency foods, particularly when grown organically. I find that organic produce tastes and smells like nature intended. The smell and taste of organic tomatoes take me back to my grandad's home-grown tomatoes. Seeing the tomatoes grow as they were nurtured gave me an appreciation of the process and the high frequency energy put into producing fruits and vegetables. Fruits and vegetables absorb energy straight from the sun. The sun carries with it light codes that will activate our dormant DNA for this point in time in our ascension process. By eating sun-drenched fruits and vegetables, you take on board the high frequency energy and light codes from the sun.

Fruits and vegetables can however, be toxic. Non-organic produce may be covered in pesticides and herbicides that may cause serious illness and hormone disruption if regularly consumed. Also, be aware of genetically modified products, as there have been many trials that have reported that they can be detrimental to human health. Some pesticides are lipid-soluble as opposed to water-soluble. This allows the pesticide to remain on the plant, even if it rains. As a result, when you ingest the produce, the lipid-soluble pesticide is absorbed and stored by your body in your fatty tissue. Over time and repeated exposure, bioaccumulation of the pesticide can occur and may cause toxic effects within your body.

You always have a choice over what you eat. Growing your own produce or buying organic is an excellent way to ensure you know what you are eating. If you are unable to do so, ensure that you regularly and safely detoxify your body and organs to remove the toxins. Many integrative medicine practitioners that offer detoxification programmes to assist with this process.

You can also use various vitamins and supplements that can assist you with detoxification at home. Below are some of the vitamins and supplements that can be effective for detoxification:

- Vitamin B3 (niacin) flush
  Vitamin B3 breaks down the fat where the toxin is stored, which in turn mobilises the toxin for excretion. This can be combined with exercise or sauna to assist in removing toxins through your skin.
- Zeolite clay and activated charcoal are chelating agents that pull the toxins out of the blood to be eliminated from the body.
- Vitamin C (ascorbic acid)
  A great source of this is white pine needle tea.

It is important to ensure that toxins mobilised in your bloodstream are eliminated from the body through the skin or gastrointestinal tract by your chosen means. If they aren't removed from the bloodstream, they will simply be reabsorbed. There are many detoxification protocols available online. I suggest that you do your own research to ensure it is safe for you, given your own personal circumstances, and if you are unsure, consult your healthcare provider.

If you choose to consume animals, you should consider the energy within the animal, how the animal has been raised, and whether it has been fed a natural, non-GMO diet. The energy and frequency of an animal that has been raised in a poor environment is notably lower than that which has been raised in a better environment through organic farming. Further to this, an animal that has lived their life in the wild has a comparably higher frequency.

It is also important to consider how the animal was slaughtered, what it was observing and what emotions it may have been feeling just before the point of death. This is important because when you eat an animal, you take the energy of that animal into your bioenergetic field.

Similarly to consuming animals, if you choose to consume fish, you should consider what toxins may be present. Our seas have become contaminated with mercury, particularly from industrial waste, which may have a detrimental effect on your health and frequency. Mercury is a heavy metal, and as such, you can use various methods to detoxify from it. This includes the previously mentioned vitamin B3 flush, activated charcoal and zeolite, as well as the consumption of coriander.

Fluoridated Water and Calcification of the Pineal Gland

Water is an integral part of your diet and, in its purest form, has many healing benefits. Unfortunately, tap water loses its life force energy responsible for the healing benefits through the water processing system. Shungite is a crystal that can be used to restore the life force energy and healing benefits of water.

Tap water is also treated with various chemicals. One such chemical present in tap water in the majority of England and many parts of the world is fluoride. Fluoride is a neurotoxin at certain levels and is a toxic industrial by-product. It can be detrimental to your health and connection to your higher self.

It has long been known that fluoride can calcify the pineal gland. The pineal gland is a small pea-sized gland that resembles a pine cone in the centre of the brain. It is responsible for your connection with your higher self, your guides and Divine Source. The pineal gland is essential for opening your third eye and inner vision, which you use for creating your outer reality. It is, therefore, necessary for your spiritual development that your pineal gland does not become calcified. A calcified pineal gland may lead to a feeling of disconnect from your higher self and confusion surrounding your life journey. Unfortunately, many water suppliers deem it necessary to fluoridate the water supply, which makes it harder to avoid. Despite this, there are certainly ways that you can remove fluoride from the water and limit your exposure to it.

One way to remove fluoride from your water is to use a water filter that removes fluoride, such as a Berkey water filter. There are many water filters available on the market that remove pollutants and toxins but do not remove fluoride. Ensure you research the water filter to confirm that it removes fluoride before purchasing. If you buy a water filter that removes everything from the water, perhaps put a pinch of Himalayan salt in the water to replace some of those essential trace elements. Distilling your water is also an option and is excellent for removing toxins. This leaves pure water at the end of the process.

There are also many tools that you can use to detoxify your body from fluoride:

- Iodine
- Chlorella
- Zeolite
- Vitamin C (ascorbic acid)
  A great source of this is white pine needle tea.
- Magnesium supplements
- Avoid toothpaste containing fluoride

In addition, there are various tools that you can use to activate your pineal gland. Firstly, sungazing is an ancient tool where you look at the sun for a few seconds and gradually build up to a few minutes over time. This should only be done during the first hour of sunrise and the last hour before sunset. During these times, the UV index is known to be near zero. The sun's energy and light codes activate the pineal gland and dormant DNA. You will know when your pineal gland is activated as you will feel a tingling sensation on your forehead between your eyebrows, where your third eye chakra is located. You may also have a heightened awareness of your senses, including foresight. In addition, fasting has been known to activate the pineal gland due to the detoxification of the body that occurs during a fast. Finally, essential oils such as frankincense, myrrh, sandalwood and rose can be used to activate your pineal gland. These can be used in a diffuser, or added to a carrier oil to be used in the bath or on your skin.

Electromagnetic Fields

Electromagnetic fields (EMFs) are areas of energy consisting of electric and magnetic fields that are invisible to the human eye. It is known that certain EMFs can destroy and denature your DNA. You can be exposed to EMFs in various ways, both in your home and external environments, and the effect of such exposure may be accumulative. Some people may be significantly sensitive to EMFs and may experience various symptoms and health issues.

As part of modern society, many of us will have items that we use daily, which emit EMFs into the environment. There are various ways that you can reduce your exposure to these EMFs in your environment. These may help to reduce any potential effects that the EMF may have on your health and frequency. Some simple ways that you can achieve this are:

- Turn electrical appliances off when they are not in use and unplug them
- Hardwire devices where possible

- Turn your mobile phone off at night time and place it over the other side of the room if it's charging
- Place your WiFi router in a faraday cage in an area of your home where you spend the least time

I believe that for every toxin that is present on the planet, there is an antidote for it. Shungite is one such antidote for EMFs. Shungite is a crystal found in Russia that has incredible properties. One of which is the ability to amplify and energise your own bioenergetic field known as your aura. This allows your bioenergetic field to negate any harmful interference from EMFs when worn on your body. Furthermore, by placing a piece of shungite on any EMF-emitting item, the potentially harmful effects are eliminated.

Finally, many plants have the incredible capability of cleansing the air of pollutants and EMFs. These plants absorb EMFs from the environment and reduce the amount you are exposed to on a daily basis. This includes many common household plants such as cacti, snake plants, spider plants, aloe vera, stone lotus flower and sunflowers.

Drugs

A drug is something that may cause physiological or cognitive changes to your body when consumed. This can be anything from pharmaceutical drugs and vaccines to recreational drugs such as alcohol. Each of these may have particular effects on your frequency and connection to your higher self. This could be an accumulative effect, such as with some pharmaceutical drugs, or an acute effect, such as with binge drinking alcohol. It is important to note that abusing any type of drug may keep you in a perpetual cycle of low frequency.

Be mindful of how you use these drugs, your intention behind their use, and your frequency at the time of use. Many drugs can affect your frequency and should not be used as a crutch when you are feeling low frequency. You should instead identify the root cause of the low frequency emotion in order to heal and allow your frequency to rise. Other drugs may affect your connection to your higher self and Divine Source. It is therefore important that you do your own research before taking any drugs, whether prescribed or not, to determine whether it has a positive or negative effect on your frequency and connection to your higher self.

21

RAISING CHILDREN TO BE MANIFESTERS

Firstly, children are natural manifesters; the key is not to erase that innate ability. They say that our children are our greatest teachers, and this is most certainly true. You need to remind your child of their innate power of creation and teach them the tools they can use to create their dream life. When you encourage them on a daily basis, you create a sense of normality surrounding their natural ability of creation.

It is essential that you do the inner healing of your own self-limiting beliefs in order to provide the best possible foundation for your child. You gain a new perspective once you have released and reframed a self-limiting belief. This is then the perspective that you pass onto your child through what you say directly to them or around them.

The most influential time in a child's life is between the ages of zero-to-seven when they are in a state of waking hypnosis. During this time in childhood, the child absorbs everything in their environment like a sponge. This is often the time when many self-limiting beliefs are created. As parents, we must be very mindful of the words that we speak to our children, the conversations that we have around them, and who we allow to take care of them. This may be at a nursery, a school, a club or a family member. Consider who you are allowing to programme your child and whether this aligns with your parenting style.

Remember that the best way to teach a child is to allow them to learn by example. If they see you offering gratitude for all that life offers, so will they. If they see you approach life as a series of experiences and lessons rather than good and bad events, so will they. Always encourage children to look for the silver lining in any situation. This will allow them to see situations from a different perspective and learn positive lessons from every situation. It is also important that children see their parents setting goals and intentions and then responding to the universal signs and synchronicities, as well as taking inspired action.

Always speak to your child in a positive and encouraging manner. Tell your child they are intelligent and capable when they are learning a new skill. Tell them they are confident, powerful, worthy, beautiful and loved. Encourage them on a daily basis, and remind them of the powerful creator that they are.

What your child repeatedly thinks and feels is what they will ultimately create in their reality. If they are worrying about something, help them to reframe it in a positive manner. Perhaps they are worried about making friends at their new school. So, reframe this by telling them they are a magnet for attracting good friends. It is also important for you as a parent to be in tune with your child. This allows you to notice if your child's frequency has dropped and have a conversation with them to find out what the contributing factor is. It is important that you help your child to acknowledge and understand their feelings so that they aren't suppressing them. You can then take action to help your child find a positive solution for the situation.

Being generous, kind and non-judgemental is another thing that children pick up on and imitate from a young age. Teach your children that it is always good to give to others, help others and be kind to others. Everything is energy, and what you give out, you receive back.

It's important that we lead by example as parents and teach our children the tools in order for them to take their power back and create a life that they love. From my experience of raising three children of my own to be the creators of their lives, I would recommend buying them age-appropriate books about manifestation and tools such as oracle cards and spell kits to open up their intuitive and spiritual side. When my children were little and going on school trips and pack holidays, I sent them with a small piece of amethyst, and they knew to call upon Archangel Michael three times for protection if they felt any low energy. They also had teddy bears that were handmade to contain specific crystals to help them throughout their childhood. Always encourage them to listen to their intuition and cultivate inner self-trust. I would also recommend encouraging your child to spend time doing what brings them joy and grounding outside in nature. You can also teach your child to use many of the tools written in this book in an age-appropriate way. Perhaps you ask them daily to list three things that they are grateful for, or spend time with them creating affirmations and sigils to stick around their bedroom. Children also have the most incredible imaginations, and asking them to visualise the end result of their goals, is an excellent way to focus their creative energy.

22

ASCENSION TO 5D CONSCIOUSNESS

We are right in the middle of the most incredible time here on earth. A shift in consciousness is taking place from the lower 3D energies of fear, anger and resentment to 5D energies of oneness, love and joy. Many of us have incarnated at this time to help raise the vibrational frequency of our beautiful planet. One way this is achieved is through the integration of light codes and high frequency energies. The central sun emits light codes that are absorbed by our bodies, and this results in upgrades to our DNA. These upgrades awaken and reactivate our dormant DNA strands. For many, this is 12 strands of DNA, but I have knowledge of individuals that have 24, 36 or 48 strands of DNA. Recently, I have also been setting the intention during meditation that all the dormant DNA strands within all the cells of my body are activated. The reactivated DNA allows our forgotten, natural abilities to manifest, such as telepathy, levitation, astral projection, bilocating, and instant creation of our realities. As we ascend into the 5D consciousness, we begin to bring our desires into our realities faster than before. The light codes are also absorbed by every aspect of nature, including the trees, soil, water and other animals. This further integrates the high frequency energies within the planet that are essential for ascension to 5D consciousness.

We are also here to raise the frequency of the collective consciousness and awaken people to their true power within. This will allow more people to ascend to the 5D consciousness. There are many important astrological events and changes in frequencies currently happening. These can be felt as intermittent, short-term physical symptoms such as extreme fatigue, ringing in the ears and vertigo. These are just a few examples of many ascension symptoms experienced by individuals as they integrate the light codes and frequencies. We have found that meditation, salt baths, and giving yourself time to rest have all been particularly helpful when we experience such symptoms.

As you are reading this book, I am certain that you are on your path of ascension to the 5D consciousness. Enjoy being here during this incredible time on earth. Spend time outside to connect to all of the energies that nature has to offer. Allow your body to absorb the light codes from the central sun. Set the intention that you call back all of your soul fragments into alignment, and take back your power. You are a powerful, multidimensional being, so step into that power and create a life you love.

Notes

Notes

Notes

Notes

Printed in Great Britain
by Amazon